Give Your Worship

How To Write Christian Songs In 1 Hour Without Forcing Inspiration

ELIAS LENGÉ

Give Your Worship

How To Write Christian Songs in 1 Hour Without Forcing Inspiration

Planning an event?

Author Elias Lengé can speak at your live event. For more information or to book Elias to speak at your next event, **email support@giveyourworship.com**

ATTENTION: CHURCHES, COMPANIES, UNIVERSITIES, COLLEGES, AND PROFESSIONAL ORGANISATIONS:

Discounts are available on bulk purchases of this book, it's associated books and video courses for educational, gift purposes, or as bonus for increasing your customer subscriptions or renewals. Special books or book excerpts can also be created to fit specific needs. For information please contact support@giveyourworship.com.

Paperback ISBN-13: 978-1-7771702-6-4
Audiobook ISBN-13: 978-1-7771702-7-1
eBook ISBN-13: 978-1-7771702-5-7

GET YOUR FREE
SONGWRITING VIDEO LESSON!

GIVE YOUR Worship

To say thank you, I created a **mini songwriting video lesson** that I would like to give to you for **FREE.**

Whether you're just getting started with songwriting or you have some experience, I created this mini course to help you get results.

TO GET YOUR FREE MINI SONGWRITING VIDEO LESSON GO TO:
Https://www.GiveYourWorship.com/**Lyrics**

Scan With Smartphone Camera To
Watch Free Songwriting Video Lesson

DEDICATION

I dedicate this book to God first, the one who gave me my talent for music and a heart of worship.

To all the teachers, worship leaders, mentors, peers and pastors who've helped me to develop into who I am today — many of you have had an impact in my life with playing instruments, writing songs, leading worship and recording music. Thank you for all the ways you have helped me; it allows me to keep growing.

And to my darling wife, Jemimah, thank you for your love, hard work and support. Without your willingness to serve me at the level that you do every day, this book would have been drastically delayed or derailed. I'm looking forward to building a bright future with you and doing for you more of the things that make you smile and cry with laughter.

CONTENTS

	Dedication	iv
	Contents	v
	Acknowledgments	vii
	About Give Your Worship	x
	Introduction	1
1	**Your Songs: Odd Without God**	7
	What is true worship?	8
	Don't worship your worship. Worship God	16
	Why worship God?	18
2	**Your #1 Songwriting Shortcut**	25
	The Music Matrix	30
	How to collaborate	40
	Flow or Frame: What's your style?	44
3	**How To Write Lyrics Part 1**	49
	The purpose of melody	50
	Major building blocks	58
	Minor building blocks	64
	The P.I.M.S method	70
	Rhyming	78
4	**How To Write Lyrics Part 2**	83
	How to use syllables	83
	The 5 categories of Christian songs	87
	The power of pronouns	97
	The 5 stages of faith	103
5	**The 7 Song Structures**	113

6	**How To Write a Hit Song**	121
	Avoid this	126
	Entering the charts	127
	Award-winning songs and chart toppers	129
7	**How To Get Inspiration Without Forcing It**	139
	What is inspiration?	140
	Where do good song ideas come from?	140
	How to get inspiration when you need it most	141
	Where do other writers get their inspiration?	143
8	**Help People To Sing Your Songs**	151
	Audio	151
	Video	159
	Lyrics, chord charts & manuscript	161
	Social Media sharing	163
9	**Criticism: What Will People Say?**	169
	Valid or void?	173
	How to tell if your song's any good?	174
10	**Good Examples and Mistakes To Avoid**	181
	Good examples	181
	Mistakes to avoid	184
11	**Putting It All Together**	187
	Secret songwriting steps to give your worship	187
12	**Your Songwriting Checklist**	197
	Closing Thoughts	201
	About The Author	202
	Your Hidden Chapter…	203
	Chord Progressions To Spark Song Ideas	205

ACKNOWLEDGMENTS

I want to start by giving a special thank you to those who I call "pivotal people" — God-sent people in my life who showed up during key moments in my journey to unknowingly teach, nudge and encourage me in the direction of eventually writing this book for you.

An extraordinary thanks to my earliest guitar teachers, Keith and Paul, and my music teachers, Mrs Bailey and Mrs Williams. Thank you for making music an engaging subject. You activated a switch inside me at a young age which has stayed on for 20 years and counting.

To my English teacher, Mrs Hodgkinson, thank you for making English such a captivating subject in secondary school. Your ability to tell stories, make Shakespeare relevant, along with encouraging me to enter my first poetry reading competition of Roger McGough's *Just Another Autumn Day*, created in me a love for wordplay that continues today. Just ask my wife; she would agree.

To Pastor David and Carol Corke, Pastor Richard and Linda Ward, and Pastor Femi and Remi Ogunrinde — you are the men and women of God who have been pastors to me at different stages of life. Thank you for always guiding me either towards or back to God.

To Andrew Chadwick, thank you for teaching me to play my first worship song, *Let God Arise*. Playing that song at Hebron Pentecostal Church was the genesis of my worship leading in churches around the world. Thank you to Pastor Prem Joseph for being a long-time music collaborator over the years; your incredible talent and humble attitude has taught me a great deal and directly adds to the results that I can produce for clients.

Thank you to my parents for buying me and my brothers our first-ever musical instruments and recording equipment. It started my curiosity for recording and led me to find recording mentors around the world.

To Dave, Twiggy and Carol, you helped me understand the technical and creative parts of recording music, and you gave me access to equipment I wouldn't have gotten anywhere else. It ignited a passion for recording that led me to earn my B.A. Honours in Music Technology from the London College of Music, which in turn opened doors for me to work at commercial studios around the world.

To the late Ralph Murphy, you taught me a perspective of songwriting I'll never forget through your songwriting workshops, book and personal correspondence. Thank you for your insight and for listening to my songs with constructive feedback during my improvement phase as a songwriter.

I want to thank Christopher Wells; you were the first person to compliment my writing before anyone else. I didn't even think I could write that well, let alone write an entire book. You have the patience of Mother Theresa, the intelligence of Stephen Hawkins, and the generosity of Santa Claus! Thank you for being my friend over the years, for the countless dinners and lunches, confidence-building pep talks, and the verbal kicks up the rear. You helped me to see the value in my experiences and knowledge before I could see it myself. It's your wisdom that gave me the final nudge I needed. Without you, this book would not have gone to print.

And lastly, to my darling wife Jemimah Lengé, you have helped me in many ways to finish this book. God knew I needed you, and he fashioned you just for me and waited until the right time to bring us together. I'm excited to live a life with you that honours Him everywhere we go. I love you.

Each one of you is a pivotal person in my music story. You led me to write this book that will help people to write songs that will, in turn, change other people's lives. Every person deserves friends and mentors like you in their life.

Thank you. I am forever grateful.

ABOUT *GIVE YOUR WORSHIP*

This book will help you to write God-focused lyrics in 1 to 3 hours consistently and achieve a standard of songwriting that you can be proud of. The passion you have inside you to write songs has probably been with you for years and probably visits you almost daily in the form of dreams and new song ideas. You may know this already, but my hunch is that those songs won't stop coming, so you need to express them.

Let this book be your guide that helps you to finish writing songs that reach people who need them most. Imagine thousands of people from around the world connecting with God because of your lyrics. This book will help you move towards that result. As an example, below are a few online comments of appreciation from people who have been impacted by songs; these songs were written by Christians who are just like you:

"This song saved me from a suicide amen." — Anil

"I am a soldier currently deployed in Europe. And it's tough. My faith is being tested daily. I want to feel the love and security of Christ and know that I am not alone in this world. I want to be on fire for Christ, spreading his word and love. I love this song. I'm glad I found it." — Christopher

"I was lost and bound by sin in complete darkness. God used this video and song on YouTube when I was alone in my room to reveal his grace through his Son to me in such a profound way, my life was changed at that moment and I was born again." — Landowar

In this book, you will learn a series of effective songwriting mindsets and techniques that will help you write God-focused lyrics in any genre. These techniques are proven over decades, are still being used today, and will continue to be used for decades to come. And that's why they'll work for you. You can cherry-pick and use just a handful of them or use them in combination to achieve more impact.

As well as helping you to stay relevant, *Give Your Worship* will show you how to be biblical in your songwriting. You don't have to use the heaviest theology to be effective, but your songs do need to draw attention away from yourself and towards God the Father, God the Son and God the Holy Spirit as well as the Bible's message of hope.

One key mindset is to write songs so well that they're good enough to be played on the radio (even if going to radio is not your goal). This mindset is a reminder back to a time when radio was the only way to listen to new music. As a radio songwriter, you needed to pass both creative and technical quality checks by the station directors before your song could be approved and played on the radio. You couldn't just scribble some lyrics on the back of a napkin and expect to be heard by thousands of people. Your songs had to have thought and craftsmanship behind them; they had to be written and rewritten; they needed a catchy melody and to be compelling to the target listeners of that radio station.

Today we live in a time where streaming is the most popular way to listen to music and services such as Spotify, YouTube, and Apple Music are more popular than radio. However, streaming services do not use the same creative and technical control checks as radio, meaning almost anyone can upload songs online. The problem with streaming is that songwriting quality has gone down as the quantity of music uploads has gone up. Low-quality writing happens when songwriters haven't learned the skills that you're about to learn. By writing to a radio standard, your songs will stand out for the right reason — excellence.

Your God-given songs matter and this book is going to be your practical guide to help you deliver those songs to listeners who need to hear them most. So let's get started.

INTRODUCTION

Do You Have Broken Beliefs?

Have these words ever been said to you? "You've either got it, or you don't." When it comes to writing lyrics, this is a false belief, and you have my full permission to break that false belief on purpose and to feel good as you break it. The pages in this book will reveal to you the truth, that writing lyrics is a skill, a skill that you can learn, improve and even teach others if that's your goal. How do I know? Because there was once a time when I had never written a song. Zero, zilch, nada. Today I have written songs that have been recorded by other artists, sung in churches, played on the radio, seen on television, performed on stages and purchased online.

What's Possible For You

My promise to you is that when you finish this book and put to practice the skills you are about to learn, you will be able to write 1, 10, 100 songs and more. I've done it from zero, so I know you will do it too. It's going to take some practice, and not just once, but fun-sized practice again and again before you notice your songwriting skills improving. I'm asking you to believe that it's possible, and believe that it's possible for you.

Here are some results that you can expect when you take massive action:

- Start and finish writing **a new song in 1-3 hours**
- Find the lyrics easier than you used to
- Know who to collaborate with, who to avoid, how to collaborate, and where to find your next collaborator
- Write lyrics that impact listeners for God
- And more

This all sounds like a big promise, but after you've finished your 3rd song, you'll be glad you took action. By the 7th song, it's going to feel even more amazing, and by the time you finish your 12th song, the skills you learn in this book will feel easier and easier to do.

Allow this book to be your writing companion a book that you come back to, again and again, to use as a checklist whether you're starting a brand new song, picking up where you left off or rewriting your lyrics as you record. Whatever your situation, this book will work for you when you work it, so keep it close.

Start Now

Also, **don't** wait for some special angel to come from heaven with a message from God, giving you permission to start writing your first song. You were made by a creator God who made you creative by nature, which means you already have permission from God to be fruitful with your gift and multiply it into as many songs as you can. Do it! Don't be crippled or paralyzed by perfectionism; stop it. Your songs don't have to be perfect, but they do have to be finished. Let me repeat that, finished is **always** better than perfect.

If you are writing for the first time, it doesn't make you a poser, fake or pretentious for wanting to write a song. So if that's your broken belief about songwriting, destroy it now. Just think about it, has anybody ever been born with 10 songs already written? No! They first learned how to write, the same way that you're about to learn. So in a way, it's less authentic to know that people need to hear your God-given songs, but you refuse to write them. Instead here's a better biblical belief: when God sends you a message to deliver, make sure you deliver that message, and yes messages can come in song form.

Finish Reading This Book

Promise yourself that you will **finish reading this whole book**. Put an end date in your calendar now of when you will finish reading this book, ideally **in the next 7 days or less**. Get the audiobook version, listen to it, immerse yourself, practice the skills, and share the ideas from this book with others who want to write songs like you do. It might surprise you to learn that many people don't finish reading books that they start. Some credible sources say that as many as 80% of people don't finish, and 90% don't make it past chapter 1, don't let that be you! Do not join the choir of complainers who sing the tired song "it doesn't work" based on giving zero effort. Be the exception, finish this whole book, put it into action, and get results. It takes less time than you'd think. One day you will run into a committed member of the choir of complainers, and you'll be able to help them to improve their songwriting because you are a doer who will finish this book and take action.

Save Your Ideas

As you learn new skills from this book, it will inspire new song ideas at random and unpredictable times. Because of that I strongly suggest either having your phone, pen, and paper (preferably all three) near you at all times to capture good ideas when they strike keep them near you even as you shower or sleep. You will be tempted many times by this thought "I'll remember it", the truth is you probably won't remember your idea, even if you have a very good memory. The very moment you get an idea, save it quickly on your phone's voice recorder, a notes app or paper. If you don't do that, your idea will start fading within 3 minutes, after 3 hours it's going to get smaller in the distance, after 3 days you'll be kicking yourself because you will have completely forgotten. So record everything, write it, capture it no matter how small, even a 10-second idea could be developed into a full song, so stay ready.

Who This Book Is for

This book is for you if you are a person with a heart of worship that wants to see God made great through music. Whether you are writing your first or your one-hundredth song, your passion in worship is to connect with and lead people to God. So, this book is for you if you are a:

- Worship Leader / Pastor
- Worship Team Member
- Christian Musician / Recording Artist
- Sunday School Teacher
- Songwriter or want to be a songwriter

If you fit into one or more of those categories, then this book is what you need. If you just want to start writing lyrics, solve your writer's block or sharpen your skills, then this book is jam-packed with action steps to speed up your success.

> **Tip:** If you don't fit into any categories above and you do not play an instrument but have a heart of worship and are willing to learn, this book has something for you too.

The techniques in this book will work in any genre like:

- Contemporary Christian Music
- Gospel Music

- Hip hop Music
- Rock Music
- Hymns (Traditional and Modern)
- Country Music
- And more

The fundamentals of good songwriting work regardless of genre and any genre can glorify God when the lyrics are biblical and written to worship Him.

Who This Book Is Not for

This book is not for you if being on stage, being seen, heard, receiving compliments and becoming famous are more important to you than God's agenda. Just walk away. Your ego can get that kind of gratification at your nearest open mic or karaoke night. Understand that those things are not wrong in and of themselves, but they should be a byproduct, not your primary pursuit. Worship is reserved only for God.

So are you excited to learn how to write lyrics? Because I'm very excited to show you how. Let's get started.

CHAPTER 1
YOUR SONGS: ODD WITHOUT GOD

Before you learn any songwriting techniques, use of pronouns, or rhyme scheme patterns, it's very important to understand that your song is not your worship. Don't jump ahead in this book to learn about techniques. If you skip this critical chapter, nothing you write will connect, and you won't understand why, so keep reading.

My Old Wrong Beliefs

If you were anything like me growing up, you probably believed (wrongfully) that worship meant singing Christian songs to God. I don't know where that silly idea came from. I wrongfully believed that the slower the song's tempo and the more reflective I felt, the more it meant that I was "worshipping" when singing that song. I also had a false belief that the faster the song's tempo and the more excited it made me feel, the more it meant that I was "praising" when singing that song. Those used to be my very misguided views about praise and worship - how wrong I was! It wasn't until much later that I learned about true worship, which has very little to do with lyrics or melody.

Who Or What Do You Worship?

It turns out that we, as human beings, worship every single day of our lives. Even people who don't believe in God worship daily; the only difference is they worship something that is not God. To prove this point, go to YouTube.com and type in these different search terms: "Hillsong Conference," "Glastonbury," "Worship Together Conference" and "Reading Festival." Look for video results at least 1-hour long in length and then watch them on mute with no volume. What you'll see is people singing together; many will have their eyes closed, and many others will have their hands lifted high in reverence. In short, you will see acts of worship in all those videos. The difference is that two of those search terms are Christian conferences where people are worshipping God, and the other two festivals are not, and anything being worshipped that isn't God is an idol.

Yes, that's right, idols are not just statues made of silver or gold; idols can be anything you worship that isn't God. The Bible also teaches multiple times about how much God hates idolatry and how much it angers Him. Do your best to be mindful of and keep yourself away from idols *(John 5:21)*. Therefore, the question isn't whether you worship or not; the real question is what or who do you worship, and how often and how intimately do you worship? To accurately answer those questions, it's useful first to answer the question: what is true worship?

What Is True Worship?

The best and simplest explanation I've heard concerning true worship is from the late Pastor Myles Munroe, who passed away in 2014. In a sermon series, pastor Munroe explained that true worship is the act of placing the **most worth** and **highest value** on God **before and above anything else** in your life. That is true worship.

Pastor Munroe continued teaching from the Bible the different facets of what it means to truly worship God. He explained that true worship is:

- **Reserved only for God** and to no other person or object *(Exod 20:3-4)*
- **To acknowledge God** as the one source of all things that was, that is, and that is to come, as well as acknowledging God as the giver of everything that you've ever had, currently have and will have in the future *(Rom 11:36, 1 Cor 8:6, Ps 24:1-3)*
- **A natural response** from you as you get to know God deeper and giving Him all the credit, expressing perpetual gratitude, placing the highest value, worth, esteem, glory and honour to Him *(1 Thess 5:16-18, Ps 50:14, Ps 100:4)*
- **To bow down** in reverence and bend yourself towards God *(Exod 20:5)*
- **To prostrate yourself** on the ground facing downwards *(Gen 17:3, Matt 26:39)*
- **To mingle** with God and to be privately and intimately engrossed with Him *(Matt 6:6, John 15:5)*
- **To entirely depend** on and surrender fully to God *(Isa 41:13, Ps 23:1-2, James 4:7, Rom 4:12)*

This list is not comprehensive. Worship also means other things, including praying, tithing, fasting, and too many other things to describe in this short book. When I first learned this, I was fascinated by how worship is a multidimensional verb and not just a nice song for Sunday morning service. This means that I am truly worshipping God when I believe in my heart, show it with my actions and speak it with my words that I place the most worth and highest value on God before anyone and anything else. The songs I write and sing are just an extension of that worship but are not the worship themselves. See the difference?

So back to the question: what or who do you worship? What do you give the most time or worth to and place the highest value on in your life? Whatever your answer is to that question, that's the name of what you worship most. If your answer isn't God, I encourage you to make the changes you need with help from your church leaders to make the answer God. Even as the author of this book, I have to remain proactive in making and keeping God number one in my life every day. It has to be a deliberate act on purpose; I can't put it on automatic pilot. When I get complacent, something else will take the number one spot away from God. Following God is a choice we must make daily. Remember, you are not alone in this; people around you will want to help.

I stress this point so much because when you understand and live it, you will truly be living a life of worship, and you won't struggle to find words or inspiration to write. Songs will just flow out of you when you know God so deeply that you can't help but worship Him for His goodness.

The Opposite of Worship

For contrast and clarity, it's also important to understand the opposite of worship. The opposite is giving credit to anything else that is not God as the source and sustainer of your blessings. This takes the honour and glory away from God, and wrongfully places it elsewhere. The opposite of worship is also:

- **Lack of gratitude** for God's blessings
- **Self-praise** for talent and accomplishment
- **Self-credit**, telling people that your success is due to being a self-made man or woman
- **Destructive pride**, such as the devil who fell because of pride; he wanted self-worship *(Isa 14:12-14)*. Instead of worshipping God, his anointing, beauty, leadership and wisdom corrupted him *(Ezek 28:17)* to think he must be worshipped.

The opposite of worship can be summarised as selfishness — the unholy trinity of me, myself and I. Selfishness is a daily danger to every Christian trying to be more God-focused. Although we fall short, there is grace for all of us.

Praise and Worship. What's the Difference?

Earlier, I mentioned how I grew up wrongfully believing three false beliefs:

1. To worship is to sing songs to God
2. Fast, exciting songs are "praise" songs
3. Slow, reflective songs are "worship" songs

I hadn't really been taught by anyone that praise and worship weren't exactly the same thing. It's actually embarrassing to think how long I had been a Christian leading worship without knowing or noticing the difference for myself.

For the purpose of helping you to write better lyrics, it's important to understand the difference between praise and worship, so that you write songs in their proper context.

So, what is the difference between praise and worship? It turns out that it has very little to do with tempo; the tempo is just a coincident of a songwriting style. The simplest way to explain the difference is when you give praise to someone; you are usually describing them; when you worship, you are usually giving credit to them.

Here are definitions and some examples:

Describe: To give an account of someone in words, including their character, their qualities and their appearance. Example: *John is big, strong and kind; John is helpful when I need him; John is loving to me.*

Ascribe: To give credit to someone else for results that you have achieved. Example: *I am rich because of John; I have everything because John provides what I need; I am able to love because John first loved me.*

Do you notice the difference? The first example describes John and his character, and the second example gives credit to John for results. It can also be said that the first example praises John, and the second example is a form of worship to John. To clarify even further, look at those two examples and read them again, but change the name from John to God to better understand the difference. Get it?

Hopefully, you now see why the misconception of uptempo and downtempo isn't always accurate, and why praise and worship are more about describing God and ascribing greatness to Him as the supreme source and sustainer of everything. Can you see how your songwriting can massively improve when you understand and use this one thing alone? Remember that **praise = describe** and **worship = giving credit.**

Odd Without God

Now that you understand what true worship is and is not, the difference between songs of praise and songs of worship, and how your songs are simply an extension of true worship but not worship themselves, you are now starting to understand how your songs become odd without God. Having songs without God is like having an extension cable without a power source, or having Wi-Fi signal without a connection, or sending a message without a recipient.

If your songs don't point to Him, they will by default start to point towards you. That's odd. Here are some reasons why you don't want songs of praise and worship pointing to you:

- You are not the source or sustainer of anything. God is
- You cannot offer salvation to those in desperate need, Jesus does

- You are not the helper of billions of people at the same time; that's the role of the Holy Spirit

In addition, any time you write a song that doesn't point to God, it can start to draw attention onto and magnify your insecurities, dysfunction and fears (can you imagine those lyrics sung at Sunday morning service, conferences and concerts?) instead of magnifying the name of the Lord. In short, make God the focal point of your lyrics.

How To Put God in Your Songs

There are two ways to put God in your songs, either explicitly or implicitly.

Explicitly literally means having one or several of these names in your lyrics: **God, Jesus, Holy Spirit, Lord,** and **King.** Alternatively, you can choose to use one or more of the Hebrew names of God in your lyrics, such as Jehovah Shalom, Jehovah Jireh, Jehovah Rapha or their English versions such as the Lord our Peace, Provider, Healer, etc. One example of a song that explicitly uses the name **Jesus** and some English versions of His Hebrew names is the song*You Are* by Kirk Franklin.

Implicitly means to imply God in your lyrics, but not directly refer to Him by name, instead, using words such as You, Him and He. You can hear an example of this in the song *How He Loves Us* written by John Mark McMillan. Later in this book, you will learn when to use the explicit or the implicit approach.

Although both the explicit and implicit approaches are valid and have a place, I personally prefer the explicit approach because there's no confusion to both Christians and non-Christian listeners about who and what the song is about. Plus, there's power in the name of Jesus, so I like to use it anytime I can. The implied approach assumes that the listener "gets it" and knows who the song is about (this is called writer's assumption), which really depends on the listener.

As a songwriter, it's important for you to understand that the implicit approach of lyric writing can cause some friction with certain listeners. The problem is ambiguity around **who** the song is written about if it doesn't explicitly mention God. In fact, there's a long-standing joke among many Christians who poke fun at certain songs because the lyrics sound like they could be a secular pop song about a romantic lover. In these songs, you could add the word "baby" and get a coherent Pop song. God is not a romantic interest, hence the friction.

However, this does not mean that you should stop using the implicit approach altogether because there is a place for it, and it does serve a purpose. It does, however, mean two things: 1) That you have to use a little more songwriting skill to avoid unexplained lyrics, which leaves too much to the imagination, and 2) That you clearly understand which audience your song will serve before you write your lyrics. These two topics will be covered in more detail in the coming chapters.

A quick solution that will help you to solve the "pop song problem" in your lyrics is to read your lyrics out loud without singing, as though you are reading a storybook. You can even record your reading on your phone or have someone else read your lyrics to you. This will reveal any lyrics that you may need to explain or rewrite.

Theology Is Your Best Friend

Theology or becoming a theologian is simply someone who chooses to study God so they can draw closer to Him, know His character better, understand His word deeper and worship Him in a more meaningful way. So I encourage you to decide to become a student of the Bible. You may be asking yourself: how do I do that?

The simple answer in four words is: **read your Bible daily.** You cannot worship what you don't know, so get to know God by reading your Bible. There are free Bible study plans you can follow step-by-step at www.bible.com that will deepen your knowledge of and relationship with God.

I also suggest that you write your lyrics with an open Bible, The Bible app, or the bible.com website for reference. Doing this one thing alone will help you in the following ways; it will:

- Make your songwriting easier because you can literally copy entire sentences from the Bible around a certain theme and use them in your song - and it's allowed
- Keep your lyrics biblical and theological
- Avoid misrepresenting God, misquoting verses, and incorrectly telling Bible stories

When you study your Bible, followed by constructive questions and discussions with friends, your Bible study group or your pastors; you'll be able to evaluate your own life experiences and identify specific times where God was helping. Doing this will help you write more theological and better songs.

You can't describe who you don't know. So when you make an effort to know God better, you'll be able to make Him known to others in a personal way. This creates testimonies for you and also serves as inspiration for new songs and creates a positive feedback loop that looks something like this:

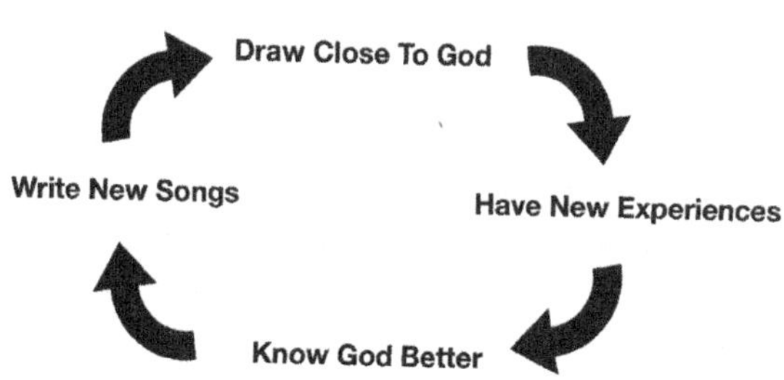

Positive feedback loop for inspiration

For biblical songwriting inspiration, I recommend that you start by exploring the book of Psalms.

DON'T WORSHIP YOUR WORSHIP

Worshipping God is a central theme to the entire Bible. Just think about it - the largest book in the Bible is Psalms, and the Hebrew name for Psalms is Tehillim, which means "praise songs." Psalms has 150 chapters and 2461 verses, which mainly focuses on praising God, and shows the most intimate encounters of people with God. The Psalms also demonstrates that God responds to us in our emotional highs and lows. This theme of worshipping God repeats from Genesis to Revelations. It's actually quite fascinating to learn about, so I encourage you to check it out and dive deep. It will make you a better writer.

Keep the Focus on God

On the topic of emotional highs, I often see a lot of songwriters and musicians getting whisked away by the emotional highs of creating and playing music that they forget to worship God. I have been guilty of this myself many times, and I have to guard against that distraction proactively. I believe the reason this happens so often is that songwriters and musicians have very pleasurable experiences when writing, playing and improvising music. Can you relate to this?

I've seen this euphoria happen with different studio clients often enough to identify a visible pattern. Because of this, I have to remind myself to keep the focus on worshipping God and not on self-gratification.

Don't Worship Your Worship

Earlier in this book, you learned that God hates idols *(Exod 20:3, 1 John 5:21)*. You also learned that anytime you ascribe greatness to something and your worship is received and accepted, that thing can become your idol. So it's possible to get caught up with the ecstasy of melody, lyrics and collaboration and become so obsessed that you put more worth on the **process** of worship, which ultimately isn't worthy; only God is worthy. Ironically, this can mean your process or the **activity** of worship can become your idol.

To underline this point, here's a question for you. Have you ever led worship at church and were going for it on stage or in the congregation, but you didn't sense the presence of God even though everything else felt "right?" I have. If you can relate to this, here's my next question — is it possible that you were more captivated by the process of worship rather than by God? If so, God knew it because He examines the heart *(Ps 44:21, Prov 21:2, Ps 139:2-23)*, and your songs may have been falling onto the deaf ears of God. So remember, don't worship your worship - worship God.

Leave Your Ego Behind

Worshipping your worship is made even worse when ego is added to the mix. I have worked with a lot of Christian and non-Christian musicians who feel way too superior because of their music and vocal talent. They don't yet understand that receiving compliments for their talent is like getting credit for something they didn't create. They haven't yet learned that they should instead transfer praise to God, the maker of their ability. The genuinely talented musicians are the humble ones, who work hard at their skill, can really play or sing at a high calibre, and still defer praise to God for every compliment they receive, which is worship.

I have learned from the wisdom of these truly talented musicians, so when someone pays me a compliment, I thank them for taking the time to find and encourage me and then I immediately pass the praise to God. Ascribing my success to God is a transfer of credit, which is worship. I encourage you to do the same, or you risk inflating your ego to the point of being delusional and too impressed with yourself.

Worship God

As you can see, it's very easy to accidentally drift from worshipping God into self-indulgence and making an idol of either your musical talent or the activity of worship. I've been guilty of this — avoid it. Remember, there is a difference between your worship and the one being worshipped. Remember, don't chase emotional highs; instead, chase the most high. Remember, don't worship your worship; worship God.

WHY WORSHIP GOD?

Worshipping God is the central theme of the entire Bible. Because of that, there are multiple instructions, encouragement and commandments to pray, praise, obey and worship God throughout the Bible. For example, the book of *Psalms 150:6* says: "Let everything that has breath praise the Lord." *Psalms 95:6* tells us: "Come, let us bow down in worship, let us kneel before the Lord our Maker" and *1 Chronicles 16:9* tells us to: "Sing to Him, sing praise to Him; tell of all His wonderful acts." There are countless other examples in the Bible instructing us to worship God, and I encourage you to research them because they will help your songwriting.

How to Worship God

The Bible not only tells us to pray, praise and worship God but also instructs us **how** to worship God. For example, *Ephesians 5:19* gives instructions that we should speak to one another with Psalms, hymns, and songs from the Spirit, and to sing and make music from our hearts to the Lord. In the book of *John 4:24,* Jesus teaches that God is Spirit, and we must worship Him in Spirit and in truth. Jesus also teaches how to pray in *Matthew 6:9-13*. Other biblical instructions include:

- Bow down in worship and kneel *(Ps 95:6)*
- Give to the needy in secret *(Matt 6:4)*
- Don't pray to be seen by others *(Matt 6:5)*
- Fast discreetly for God *(Matt 6:17-18)*
- Worship together and encourage other believers *(Matt 18:20, Heb 10:25, 1 Cor 14:26)*

There are many other verses in the Bible instructing us as believers about how we are to worship. I encourage you to grab your bible and make yourself more familiar with these and other verses. It will help to make you a better songwriter.

You Benefit When You Worship

The Bible also lists the benefits you receive when you worship God. In *Exodus 23:25-26,* the Bible says "Worship the Lord your God, and His blessing will be on your food and water. I will take away sickness from among you, and none will miscarry or be barren in your land. I will give you a full life span." That is an incredible Bible passage that deserves more attention. When you choose to worship God with a sincere heart of faith, even though your feelings or situation are not ideal, God sets in motion things that can only be seen in the spiritual that will bless you. Even more benefits are available when you worship God:

- God will draw near to you *(James 4:8)*
- Draws men closer to God *(John 12:32).*
- Delivers you from your enemies *(Ps 18:3)*
- Invites God's presence *(2 Chr 5:11-14)*
- Brings you victory *(2 Chr 20:15-20)*
- Blesses your family for 1,000 generations because you love God and keep His commands *(Exod 20:6)*

There are too many other benefits to name for worshipping God, but one thing that is obvious through all these biblical examples is that worship is for your benefit, not God's.

Worshipping Idols (No, No, No!)

The Bible also details for us many, many times that God hates idols and that we are to avoid idolatry **proactively**. I can't state this enough - God hates idols! This is emphasised in *1 John 5:21, Colossians 3:5* and *Exodus 20:3-6*. In fact, the Bible teaches that idolatry is such a sin in God's eyes that:

- All who make idols are nothing *(Isa 44:9)*
- They'll suffer more and more *(Ps 16:4)*
- They turn away from God's love *(Jonah 2:8)*
- They pollute themselves *(Ezek 20:31)*
- God will be against them *(Lev 20:1-9)*
- They provoke God's anger *(Deut 32:16)*
- They hate God, and their children will be punished to the 3rd and 4th generation *(Exod 20:5)*

The Bible clearly details the dangers and curse of idolatry. So, please make sure that as a songwriter, you create songs from a heart of wanting to worship God and that you keep yourself away from idols, pride and self-worship.

If you find yourself writing songs or leading worship because you want to be famous or you believe you're the best musician and should, therefore, be the "obvious choice", I encourage you to stop immediately. Take some time away with God to get your heart right, correct your attitude and make your gift, talent, and anointing about God and leading people to Him. This will orient your mind and heart to worshipping God for the right reasons.

Congratulations! If you read the book from the start to this point, it means that you have gone further than 90% of people who started reading, which also means that you are for real. It only gets better, so let's go a little deeper.

KEY POINTS FROM YOUR SONGS: ODD WITHOUT GOD

We all Worship Daily

Worship is when we acknowledge, prioritise, place the most value on, or give worth and credit to someone or something, so even non-believers worship.

Your Song Is Not Your Worship

True worship is how you live. Your song is just an extension of your worship.

Worship Is A Multidimensional Verb

Worship is an action word. We are instructed, encouraged and commanded as believers to live a life of true worship to God.

Praise and Worship Are Different

Praising God is to describe him. Worshipping God is to give Him all credit for all your blessings.

Your Songs Are Odd Without God

Your song without God lacks purpose, significance and impact. You risk it being about you.

Your Songs Have a Purpose

The purpose of your song is to worship God and help lead other people to also worship.

Don't Worship Your Worship. Worship God

Don't make the **activity** of playing instruments, songwriting and singing into your **idol**. As a songwriter, be mindful of the euphoria. Don't chase emotional highs. Chase the most High.

Include God in Your Songs

If your songs fail to point to God, your songs will point to you. That's odd.

There Are Benefits to Worshipping God

The Bible instructs us to worship God and lists benefits when we worship. Learn more about the benefits of your worship.

There Are Curses to Idolatry

Run away from idolatry. Proactively avoid your songwriting and worship being about fame, fortune or pride; it can become your idol.

Have a Heart of Worship

Make your songwriting and worship about God and leading people to Him.

CHAPTER 2
YOUR #1 SONGWRITING SHORTCUT

If you use the approach you are about to learn in this chapter, you will be able to write songs faster. If you don't use this collaboration approach, although you'll still be able to write songs, they'll take you longer to finish, and you'll experience the predictable frustration and confusion that can easily be avoided.

What Is Collaboration?

Collaboration is when two or more people work together to create a shared desired result. This simple definition of collaboration can be broken down into three parts:

1. Two or more (People)
2. Working together (Process)
3. Towards a shared desired result (Purpose)

Why Collaborate?

Short Answer: it works! A 2012 study on collaboration by Stanford University revealed that people who collaborated stayed on task 64% longer than people who worked alone. The study also found that people who collaborated enjoyed higher engagement, lower fatigue levels, and higher success rates. These kinds of positive results are available to you when you choose to write songs in collaboration with the right people.

I believe the reason collaboration works so well is because we thrive off each other. As human beings, we excel in community and do our best when we are around other people. So simply knowing that you are a part of a team working on a task will motivate you more to take on your songwriting challenges. Remember, the key to successful collaboration is to clearly communicate and agree with your writing partner about the result you want for your song.

Although I don't have the data to back this up, I've observed for many years that when it comes to collaboration, what may feel like a fully formed idea might only be half the final sound. The other half of your idea is (often unknowingly) in the mind of your collaborator. When the two halves meet, music magic can happen with incredible sounding results — so finding the right people matters.

Famous examples of collaborations include Matt Redman and Jonas Myrin, who together wrote the songs *You Alone Can Rescue*, *Our God,* and *10,000 Reasons.* Other notable collaborations include Joel Houston, Matt Crocker and Salomon Lighthelm, who wrote the song *Oceans*, and the song *Who You Say I Am* was written by Rueben Morgan and Ben Fielding.

Hopefully, these examples of well-written worship songs help you to see the writing results that are available to you when you work with the right people and why collaboration is your number one songwriting shortcut.

Collaboration Ground Rules

Before you start collaborating, it's essential to communicate and agree on some basic ground rules with your writing partners. Ground rules will create understanding, respect, harmony, results, and also help to avoid creative tension. Your ground rules may look different from the ones below, but start with these and change them to fit your own needs. The collaboration ground rules to follow are:

1. God first

This one is obvious; start your songwriting session with prayer and put God at the centre. Make sure your song worships Him and avoids self-glorification, which is an easy thing to do when you lose perspective of who's important. Drive and steer your spirit in the direction of worshipping God at all times as you write. Do this as many times as you need to, and your song will also help others to worship God.

2. Have fun

As you write your songs, it's literally called "playing" music, meaning you have full permission to be in a state of play. So if you're not having fun, something went wrong somewhere. Fix it.

3. Choose your environment

Write in an environment that inspires good musical and lyrical ideas. It might be your home, the outdoors, or at church — wherever you hear God the most, feel His presence and feel inspired.

4. Fight fair

This ground rule is SUPER-important: don't fight your collaborator. Instead, fight (playfully) for the best ideas. Arguments usually happen between collaborators when you or your writing partner have not yet learned the skill of detaching yourself from your ideas. As a result, any suggestion to improve an idea might feel like a personal attack when it's not. Resist the urge to argue. Stay objective and listen to your collaborator comments that could improve one or more aspects of your original ideas.

5. Test your ideas

This ground rule exists just in case you and your writing partner don't agree on which idea is best. In this situation, you may find it useful to create two versions of the same song — one with ideas you agree on and another with ideas you don't agree on. Doing this will give you the ability to test your songs more objectively. Remember, the purpose of your song is not to contain as many of your ideas. The purpose of your song is to praise and worship God and lead other people to do the same. So don't choose ideas just because they're yours; choose ideas that support the purpose.

6. You are an equal

If you wish to make your song commercially successful and make an effort to do promotion and marketing, or if your song earns money, it's essential to agree on ownership of the song. Personally, I don't like to start writing collaborations with this tone, but it is important to address. The key point to understand about copyright or songwriting credit is that the law makes it easy for you and automatically assumes equal ownership of your song by default.

7. Keep it simple

What this means for you is that you have 100% ownership of a song if you wrote it alone. If two people write a song, the law gives 50% equal ownership. If three people write a song, the law gives 33.3% equal ownership. If four people write a song, the law gives 25% equal ownership, etc. This also applies if one person writes all the lyrics and the other writes all the melody, both have equal ownership because the melody that makes the song successful is equal to the lyrics that people enjoy, one can't exist without the other. Therefore, in the eyes of copyright laws, both writers have equal ownership of the song.

In some cases and in the spirit of goodwill, songwriting credit is given to a person for being present during the session and making editorial suggestions to add, remove or reorganise words. Even though they technically didn't write any lyrics, their input lead to the end result of a successful song. This is becoming a growing trend around the world.

You may choose for equal ownership to change. In that situation, all writers should agree to different percentages and put that agreement in writing. So make your writing session fun by getting straight into creative mode and start each collaboration with a shared and agreed-upon understanding of ownership like the law suggests.

Is that an oversimplified version of copyright law? Yes, I simplified it on purpose. It may vary (a little bit) from country to country, but for the most part, it holds true.

The Magic Unicorn

For whatever reason THIS area of songwriting (copyright/credit) more than any that I can think of makes people behave in uncomfortable and uneasy ways. It's almost as though some songwriters believe that EVERY song they write WILL become a MONSTER hit with 7 billion streams. It's as though that song will make a lot of money, which will produce for them a magic unicorn that will fly them to an exclusive planet where the ONLY weather forecast every single day is heavy showers of royalty cheques with a chance of millions. As a result, some songwriters don't want to share fairly or at all.

The truth is a lot of songs experience only a modest amount of success with quite small amounts of money that come from multiple sources like streaming, purchases, downloads and others.

Lessons that I've learnt from my personal experiences have led me to avoid songwriting with people who believe in magic unicorns. The way to identify unicorn believers is that they start collaborations with talks of copyright and ownership. The die-hard believers may even give you an agreement to sign before collaboration can begin. Signing agreements is not bad per se; but to me, it feels like pouring water on the wood before lighting a fire. It's a token of distrust that doesn't create ideal conditions to collaborate, and it kills the creative fire fast.

It's your choice whether you write with unicorn believers or not. The law makes it easy and assumes equal ownership for you. If a songwriting agreement has to be in writing; a single one-page one-side document is all you need.

Having these 7 ground rules will help your collaboration to stay focused, less biased to your ideas and more biased towards the best ideas, as well as simplifying what ownership looks like. This leaves you to focus on the main thing, writing a song that people want to listen to on repeat at least three times daily.

THE MUSIC MATRIX

With your songwriting ground rules firmly in place, you will next need to find 1 or 2 people as collaborators. I believe if it's your first time collaborating or you're a first-time songwriter, you should focus on finding just 1 collaborator because 2 partners may be too many too early. As you develop the right collaboration mindset, experiences, and results, you can later include a second or third writing partner. But to begin with, start with one.

If you're wondering how many is too many? I believe the maximum number for a lyric writing collaboration to be a maximum of 3 people per song. I think this because I subscribe to the idea that a machine with fewer moving parts is easier to fix and maintain when things break down. This idea can also be applied to writing lyrics; a song with fewer collaborators is easier to fix and rewrite when a song breaks down. Any more than 3 can become a crowd and increases the likelihood of creative differences and tensions that can lead to arguments, it's best to avoid this from happening. Ultimately you will decide what number works best for your collaborations, but for me when it comes to writing lyrics, 3 is the magic number.

So who are the right people, who should you collaborate with and who should you avoid? If you're anything like I use to be, you may want to collaborate with anyone who has a little free time and is willing to get together. Collaborating with anyone is a mistake you should avoid because my years of experience has revealed to me that different musicians will have different tendencies/strengths that can help or hurt your song's chances of success. So whatever music tendencies you have, you need for your collaborator to have opposite and complementary tendencies so that you write and finish more songs.

I put these music strengths in a simple table that I call the "Music Matrix". The Music Matrix helps you to identify quickly at a glance where you are most skilled and where you need more experience. You can then use that information to collaborate with the right person who compliments you where you are not as skilled. It's like a matchmaking service for songwriters.

The Music Matrix Explained

The music matrix was created to help you quickly identify two things, 1) Identify where you are musically strong and 2) Identify the strengths needed in a potential collaborator that compliment your music weaknesses. This matrix is not intended to be an absolute grid of "good" or "bad"; it works more like a spectrum showing you one or more strengths or tendencies that you may have at the same time. No one is perfect, so you won't be 100% strong in all areas of music, that's why strategic collaboration will help you massively. So remember; collaborate with someone who compliments your music weakness with their music strengths.

	A	B	C	D
1 Lyrics	Not Yet Known	Start Lyrics Easily	Finish Lyrics Easily	Start & Finish Lyrics Easily
2 Melody	Not Yet Known	Start Melody Easily	Finish Melody Easily	Start & Finish Melody Easily
3 Play this # of Instruments	0	1+	3+	5+
4 # of Songs Completed	1+	30+	70+	100+
Level	**Novice**	**Beginner**	**Intermediate**	**Advanced**

The Music Matrix

Music Matrix Columns Explained

The Music Matrix has four horizontal rows of songwriting categories labelled by name, and four vertical columns of songwriting strengths labelled A-D alphabetically. The further down the alphabet you go, the more likely your strength/experience increases in that category. So the letter D is the strongest column, which gradually decreases down to A for beginners.

So as an example, if you are good at finishing lyrics that have already been started, you'd be strong in the C1 category labelled "Finish Lyrics Easily". However, if you struggle to start new lyrics, you would be weak in the B1 category labelled "Start Lyrics Easily". Therefore your collaboration strategy should be to write with someone who's strong in the B1 category. Between your collaborator's strength to start and your strength to finish, you'll be able to write many songs together because both your strengths compliment very well. Here's a closer look at each column of strength;

Column A:

People in column A are typically brand new to songwriting and may have written none or just a few songs in the past. Those that haven't yet started writing are usually procrastinating because of their uncertainty and fears. They do not yet know their music strengths and what they need most is for their collaborator to kickstart their bottled-up passion into action. If you identify most with being in column A, then you probably have the most questions of how to start, what the process is etc., that's okay. The coming chapters in this book will answer your questions, clarify any songwriting misconceptions and simplify what to do next to write your song, so keep reading.

As a songwriter in column A, you are likely to know and have the easiest access to others in column A. My suggestion for you is to avoid musicians in column A because they may not have the experience to help guide you to the result you want. On the other extreme, column D writers may be too advanced and confuse you with too many concepts you haven't yet learned, which might leave you feeling overwhelmed into even less action. So, I recommend that you collaborate with musicians in Column B, and maybe C. The reason for this is because they'll have a little more experience than you to help you get started and push you to grow into a Column B or C writer faster than they did. Proximity is Power. If you have songs that you have started and finished, well done, that's a great achievement already. You will benefit from getting constructive feedback from more experienced writers in column C or D.

Column B:

Songwriters/musicians in column B are either able to start new lyrics, new melodies or both easier than most people. They usually play an instrument and have written 30 songs more or less (this number isn't exact, it's an estimate to help you gauge potential collaborators). Their strength is the ability to generate new ideas fast. They are often some of the most inspiring musicians to be around because their ideas never seem to stop, which can rub off on others during writing sessions. Their ideas can take the form of lyrics, song titles, stand-alone verses, fun phrases and catchy choruses recorded on their phone, notebook, receipts, scrap paper etc.

If you identify most with this column, then you are an activator, most characterised by your ability to start. You probably have a lot of ideas come to you daily, sometimes too many to keep up with and that's why you struggle to finish what you start. It's not your fault you're just overwhelmed by your strength, which can be harnessed for maximum results.

It would be wise of you to avoid other column B "starters" or "activators" as your collaborators. Working with too many column B musicians will only produce bigger heaps of unfinished ideas, which can make you feel that progress is not being made. The best person for you to collaborate with is someone in column C, maybe column D. Between your ability to start and the finishing strength of a column C writer, you'll be able to complete the most amount of songs. When working with a column C writer, you need to resist the urge to abandon a song in progress that "seems" to have hit a dead-end and instead work with the strength of the finisher even if you could have created seven new ideas in the time needed to finish. You'll be glad that you were patient enough to wait, the reward for your patience will be a finished song and establishing a writing rhythm that can speed up future songs. If you have songs that you have started and finished, well done! Get some feedback from a more experienced writer in column D.

Column C:

Musicians in column C are natural finishers; their strength is the ability to take a song already in progress and finish it with their writing partner. They are willing to stay patient and sometimes can stay stubborn too long with a song that should be left and returned to later with a fresh perspective. Their weakness is a tendency to struggle to start new ideas. They struggle to find the words to express what they feel or the music notes that start the song; they don't want to be misunderstood or choose incorrect words, so they'll stick with it longer than a "starter" will until they find just the right lyric.

If you identify more as a finisher in column C, then your natural collaborators are B column songwriters/musicians, the starters and activators of new ideas. Your ability to complete a task is one that a "starter" needs very much. The two of you may choose to collaborate on a brand new song together or on any one of the many songs your B column collaborator started and has not yet finished. As a tip, if you choose to work on an existing idea, ask your column B collaborator for their best and most recent song to work on, doing this will make use of his/her current excitement about that song to make them want to finish it.

As a C column musician, you should avoid other C columns musicians. By now, your writing experiences have probably revealed to you that you are better at finishing ideas. Therefore it would not be beneficial to work with another "finisher" if they struggle to start ideas as you do. As an alternative, you may want to consider working with a column A musician. The fresh perspective and raw talent of someone starting out could be the inspiration you need to nurture that song to finish while getting an opportunity to mentor a beginner.

Column D:

Writers in column D are usually advanced songwriters and can be labelled as a "hybrid", meaning they can start, develop and finish a song by themselves with lyrics and melody. Once they finish writing a song, they can objectively step back and say if it's good or bad and then rewrite where needed. The ability to do this usually comes from writing many songs for years, either alone or with other people. This objectivity comes from borrowed wisdom of past collaborations as well as creative intuition to take a song to completion.

A weakness for column D writers is that they tend to go to their "tried and tested" writing techniques too often. Although this is a good approach to producing consistent writing results, it can also result in a feeling of creative frustration, which feels to them like they "write the same thing" or that they're in a rut. At this stage, it is typical for column D writers to want to shake things up a little bit and get new inspiration.

If you identify most as a column D writer, you may want to avoid working with column A writers unless you detect an early talent and are willing to be patient enough to get involved and mentor him or her. The reason for this is because as an advanced songwriter with years of experience, you may forget how much you've improved and may overwhelm a new writer with your logical leaps of knowledge, which can create gaps in the understanding of a beginner. Otherwise, your natural collaborators would be a songwriter in column D and column C.

If you need new inspiration, you may want to consider writing with a writer from column B in a genre that's different from your primary genre.

Beyond Column D:

After column D, you will find songwriters and musicians who are experts, professionals and world-class talent. They too will have the same strengths and weakness listed on the music matrix, what makes them different will be:

- **Duration**
  Years spent writing, recording, touring and leading worship
- **Scale**
  Number of people reached per event (both online and offline events) either presently or throughout their career
- **Occupation**
  Full-time living earned through their music
- **Fame**
  Level of recognition in their music genre, language, countries and accolades

Your Music Matrix Shortcut

The music matrix is fast and easy. Here's how to use it in 5 steps and 5 minutes to find your next writing collaborator;

	A	B	C	D
1 Lyrics	Not Yet Known	Start Lyrics Easily ✗	Finish Lyrics Easily	Start & Finish Lyrics Easily
2 Melody	Not Yet Known	Start Melody Easily ✓	Finish Melody Easily	Start & Finish Melody Easily
3 Play this # of Instruments	0	1+ ✓	3+	5+
4 # of Songs Completed	1+ ✗	30+	70+	100+
Level	Novice	Beginner	Intermediate	Advanced

The Music Matrix shortcut

Step 1:

Put check marks next to your creative strengths, at least one per rows 1-4.

Step 2:

Put cross marks next to your creative weaknesses at least one per rows 1-4.

Congratulations! You now know what strengths your collaborator should have.

Step 3:

Join the "Give Your Worship" Facebook group, which was created with this book to help you find collaborators.

Step 4:

In that Facebook group, create a post introducing yourself and list the strength you're looking for and what genre you'd like to write in.

Step 5:

Arrange a time to collaborate with one or more people who respond to your post.

> **Tip:** Your goal should be to finish a song in 1-3 hours. So schedule either one 3-hour writing session, two 1-hour 30 minutes writing sessions or three 1-hour sessions.

Congratulations! You now have your next collaborator for your song, and you also know where to go to find future collaborators in multiple genres.

The 4 Cs of Collaboration

As well as using the music matrix, you may want to use the 4 C's of collaboration, something I learned from Author John C. Maxwell. The music matrix helps to pair you by skill, whereas the 4 Cs of collaboration helps to pair you based on the potential to get along. The 4 Cs are:

1. **Chemistry** is about personality and relationship. Do you like each other as people, and is there potential for you to get along? This is important because you may be spending a lot of time together.

2. **Commitment** is about willingness. Are you committed at the same level as your writing partner? The minimum commitment should be at least 3 hours to complete writing one song. Anything beyond that is a bonus for you both.

3. **Capacity** is about ability. Do you have the capacity needed for the writing session? Hint: using the music matrix correctly, helps to make you a strong and capable group. So the answer is yes, you are willing and able.

4. **Compliment** is about giving and taking. Do you stay open to being positively impacted by your collaborator and receive constructive feedback as well as give the same in return?

If you answered no to all four questions, choose a different collaborator. If the answer to all four questions is yes, then you owe it to yourself to collaborate now.

If your collaboration chemistry doesn't start on the first song, don't give up on that collaboration. Allow for at least three songs written together before deciding if to continue collaborating or to find new writing partners.

Now that you know collaboration is your number one songwriting shortcut, why it will work for you, who to collaborate with and avoid, and where to find your next collaborator, you are now ready to learn how to collaborate.

HOW TO COLLABORATE

Use the music matrix shortcut

Find 1 or 2 ideal collaborators by using the five steps of the Music Matrix shortcut mentioned earlier.

Before your writing session, agree on what kind of song to write

The different types of songs you can write will be covered in the coming chapters, so keep reading.

Schedule your session

Your goal should be to finish every song you write in 1 to 3 hours. It doesn't have to be "perfect" (there's no such thing); it does, however, have to be **finished**. Your writing session/s can either be:

- **One** 3-hour writing session. Finish your song to the 100% mark
- **Two** 1.5-hour writing sessions. Finish your song to the 50% mark per session
- **Three** 1-hour writing sessions. Finish your song to the 33% mark per session

> **Tip:** Keep yourself and your collaborator accountable. Your goal should be to finish each song within 7 days and in no longer than 3 weeks.

From these three options, choose whatever is practical for you and your collaborator with the goal of finishing each song in 1 to 3 hours. Set 3 uninterrupted hours aside just to write and finish an imperfect song because great songs aren't written; great songs are rewritten. If you choose to complete your song over 2 or 3 writing sessions, schedule the following session before your current session ends. You should also finish the whole song inside of a 7 day period. That way, you keep momentum on your side to finish your song.

Arrive ready and destroy distractions

You should both show up to your writing session with at least two 10-second song ideas; you'll learn more about creating melody ideas in chapter 3. This increases the chances that you'll both like one of the ideas to develop further. Make sure that all phones, notifications, pings, buzzes, and texts are off during your session, so you don't get distracted or disturbed. It's hard work for your brain to modulate between creative writing to urgency, social media to melody, work emails to lyrics, etc. In fact, the University of London did a study to look at changes in people's IQ when multitasking and found that IQ does decrease for men and women during distractions. So anything with an on button should be in do not disturb mode.

Start with prayer

The main thing is to keep the main thing as the main thing — and the main thing is God. So start every songwriting session in prayer and dedicate your song to the Lord your God.

Stay open to receive feedback

Some songwriters are so close to their idea that any constructive feedback can sting like an insult. They believe their idea is the perfect baby that never cries, poops or pees. This causes them to be closed off to rewrite any part of the song, which doesn't help. Stay open to receive constructive feedback to improve the song.

Stay open to being impacted by others

This concept took me a while to truly understand because it is counterintuitive. But when you allow yourself to be impacted by others, it gives you the ability also to impact other people. I'll repeat that: to impact people, you must first be impacted.

Be open to ideas from someone else

Some people don't accept ideas that they didn't come up with. They may describe themselves as "open-minded" in conversation until an idea from someone else arrives, and then they close up fast. Don't collaborate with closed gates, or you will shut out great ideas for your song.

Stay open to other people's approaches

Here are some questions to ask your collaborator, as well as answer yourself. These questions can be used before and during your writing session so that you are both on the same page:

- Are you open to collaborating?
- Is it okay if I ask you a few questions?
- Is it okay if I give you feedback as we're writing?
- Is it okay if I make suggestions?
- Is it okay if I make requests?

They act like phrases to kickstart constructive discussions about good ideas, so use these phrases as often as possible.

Don't force it

"Off days" do happen — not all the time, but they do come. So if you and your collaborator are both experiencing writer's block, don't force inspiration. Instead, go for lunch, take a walk and talk with each other about what God is doing in your lives, and what miracles you've witnessed lately. Speak about what exciting things are happening at your church, encourage each other's faith, share what you're reading in the Bible that is impacting you and what you're grateful for. Take some time to connect; this builds a strong foundation for good songs to happen.

Online

These collaboration steps will work for you both online and offline. To help you to collaborate easier online, I created for you the "Give Your Worship" Facebook group, a growing community of Christian songwriters from around the world. Facebook also has free video and audio chat features that will let you connect with anyone anywhere in the world. Amazing.

Your Songwriting Hacks

- Use pen and paper to write, even if your handwriting, spelling and grammar are "terrible". It's faster.
- Avoid writing lyrics on your phone during your writing session; your thumbs are slower than your ideas. You can't type as fast as you can write or sketch, plus texts, emails and notifications will distract you, your battery may die, and you may not have saved your idea and end up losing three hours of music magic.
- Take a picture of your written lyrics on your phone as a secondary backup in case you lose your songwriting book or piece of paper.
- Always use your phone's audio recorder app or a small sound device to record even your shortest melody or lyric idea as fast as humanly possible. Don't mislead yourself; you won't remember it "later" or "tomorrow." Humming, whistling or sounding the melody out with your mouth is faster than going to find your instrument and forgetting it on your way, so record your voice.

- Arrive with 100% charged devices, including your phone, laptop and voice recorder to all your writing sessions.
- If typing on your laptop, save your song in the Cloud using free services like Dropbox, iCloud or Google Drive as a secondary backup that you can access on multiple devices. It will also help to label, date and save each version of your lyrics as you add or remove ideas.
- Try writing with a different instrument in a different key or location than you'd normally use. This is the easiest inspiration available to you.
- Write where inspiration comes easiest to you either at your church, in your home, by the lake, or other locations. Mix it up.
- Bookmark or download these websites and apps. **bible.com** to quickly reference Bible verses as you write, **rhymer.com** to help generate words that rhyme with any word you type into it, **dictionary.com** to help find the meaning of a word and **thesaurus.com** to help find a different word that has the same or a similar meaning.

FLOW OR FRAME

Do you "flow" or "frame?" As you and your collaborator are writing a new song, you may find that you write more naturally in 1 of these 2 styles. The difference between the two is either planning or just plunging straight in. Here's an explanation of what both mean so you can recognise them in yourself and your writing partners.

If flow is more your natural writing style, an idea, melody or phrase may come to you, and you flow with it. You start to sing it. You pick up a pen or an instrument and create whatever flows out of you without stopping to edit yourself. You may not know what you're going to write about, and if you do, you only have a vague idea of what direction a song might take, and you're okay with not knowing. You don't want to interrupt the process until the flow slows down naturally and eventually stops. Typically you also don't want others to interrupt you either because it can be hard to get back into a state of flow if stopped prematurely. You are inspired and don't want to give any thought yet to structure, syllables, arrangement, or any form of rigidity. It just slows you down, so you write until you finish. Only then can editing start, does this sound like you? If so, your writing style is to flow more often than not. If this doesn't sound like you, your style may be to frame.

If frame is more your natural writing style, you typically want to structure your ideas, arrange them in a sequence and organise your thoughts as a way of getting started. You like to know what the song is going to be about and plot the beginning, middle and end before you write. You are likely to stop mid-flow to edit your progress and change the order of things to match your original plan. You operate best when you know the desired result, with guidelines, steps, process, arrangement, rules and sequence. Does this sound like you? If so, then your natural writing style is to frame more often than not.

The truth is, we all have a blend of both and can switch between flow when writing one song to frame when writing a different song, and that's okay. Both planning and plunging are valid approaches that work, and it's good to be aware of them, so you know how to complement your style and the style of your writing partner.

Follow these steps to give your collaborations the highest possible chance of success.

KEY POINTS FROM YOUR #1 SONGWRITING SHORTCUT

Collaboration Is Your Number 1 Songwriting Shortcut

Collaboration is when people work together through a process for a purpose. Your songwriting is a process with a purpose.

Collaboration Works

Collaboration will help you to write 64% longer maybe more. It helps you continue when others would quit.

Finish in 1 to 3 Hours

Your goal should always be to finish a song in 1-3 hours. This can be one 3-hour session, two 1.5-hour sessions, or three 1-hour sessions. Finish a song in 7 days or less and no more than 3 weeks.

Use the Music Matrix Shortcut

Who you write with can make or break your song. Use the steps in the Music Matrix Shortcut to quickly find the right collaborator for you.

Use the Collaboration Ground Rules

The purpose of ground rules is to create respect, harmony and results between you and your collaborators. This produces excellent songs and great chemistry.

Collaborate Offline and Online

You can collaborate with other Christian songwriters and readers of this book online in the "Give Your Worship" group on Facebook. That group was created as your collaboration resource for this book. You can also collaborate offline in your local area.

Collaborate Correctly

Learn to give and take when collaborating. Stay open to receiving ideas from your co-writer as well as giving ideas.

Different People Write Differently

Some writers have a style to "flow" without a defined structure, and some like to "frame" their ideas, and write with highly defined parameters. Both approaches work for different people. Remain patient when writing with a style that is opposite to yours. They both ultimately lead to great songs when given the space to grow.

CHAPTER 3
HOW TO WRITE LYRICS PART 1

HOW TO CREATE A MELODY

Melody is the essence of music. Although the primary focus of this book is to help you to write God-focused **lyrics,** there is an equal need for you to understand the function of melody in your song. You don't have to be a world genius at creating a melody, but you do need to have a basic grasp on melody to be effective when writing or when working with musicians.

Imagine a grand piano; it's easy to become overwhelmed when you think of all 88 keys. How do you create a melody with so many notes? The simple truth is a grand piano **only** has 12 notes (7 white notes and 5 black notes) — no more, no less.

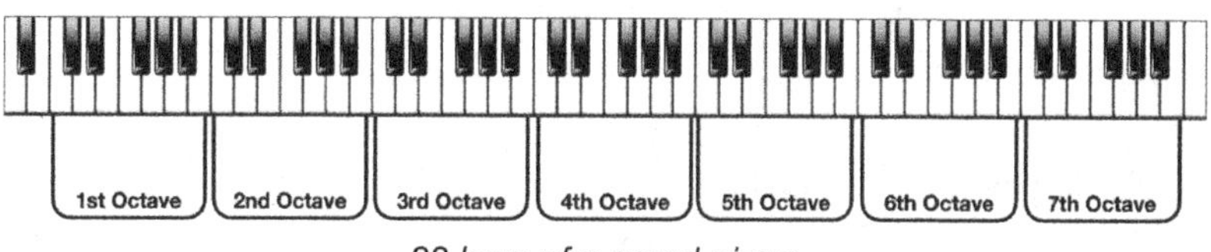

88 keys of a grand piano

These 12 notes get repeated 7 times (and a bit) to make up the 88 keys. Some notes repeat higher in pitch, and some notes repeat lower in pitch. Each time a new group of 12 notes repeat, that's called an octave above or an octave below. All of a sudden, melody becomes simple when you can reduce 88 notes down to only 12.

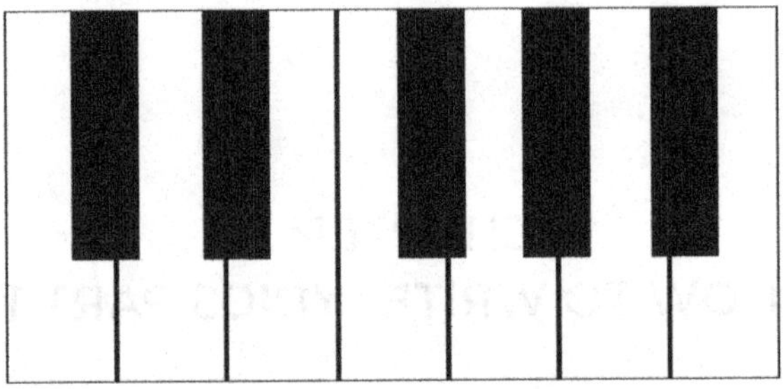

12 simple notes to create your melody

Even more straightforward than 12 notes, you can easily create your entire song's melody using between 5 and 7 notes in one octave; it's simple. If you want to get fancy, you can add more notes and a second octave, but I don't recommend adding a third octave because most people don't sing well and only have an octave to an octave and a half singing range. A comfortable 5 to 7 notes in one octave will help people feel confident in being able to sing either alone or in a group. In other words, keep your melodies simple and engaging so that people embrace them quickly.

Melodies get even simpler when writing songs for Sunday school, where you can create 4-note melodies for children to learn, remember, sing, and enjoy.

The Purpose of Melody

The purpose of melody is to invite listeners in so they want to listen longer. Once your listeners accept your compelling invitation to listen, your melody should work with your lyrics as it rises and falls within that singable 5 to 7 note range punctuating the power of your message. The melody should change and develop with your lyrics in each major and minor building block (building blocks will be explained shortly in this chapter).

By rising and falling to punctuate the lyrics, your melody sets the song up to deliver the "hook" (often the last line of lyric in your chorus). I'll repeat that: the melody should fit your hook perfectly like a hand in glove (you will learn more about hooks in the following pages). Remember, although your melody may draw listeners in, it's the quality of your lyrics that engages and makes people want to stay and listen to your song on repeat and add it to their playlist as a part of their daily routine. You're about to learn how to write relevant lyrics in the coming chapters.

If you don't play an instrument and you don't yet have a handle on melody, that's okay; go back and look at the **Music Matrix**. As a non-musician songwriter, you don't have to suddenly become a melody theory master. Simply collaborate with someone who's already good with melodies as noted in column B or D of the Music Matrix; they probably want to collaborate with you, too.

A Melody That Connects

A good melody is powerful! When done right, a melody will communicate what your song is about without a single word. The melody will already have a message or a mood, and instantly connect with a listener, also moving them in the attitude of praising and worshipping God. Because melody can communicate without words, it's understood in every language. It's like watching comedy videos by Mr Bean or Charlie Chaplin; they're funny in every language because they communicate without words. As a result, those videos produce laughter in every country where people watch them.

In the same way, when you create your melody right, even people who don't speak your language will understand what you're saying and will be able to connect with God through your song. Some listeners will take it a step further and translate your lyrics into their language because of a good melody, or you can have your song translated into multiple languages to reach more people for God.

Here are some examples of successful songs to show you that melodies can be super-simple. The melody in *Amazing Grace* has survived for more than 200 years using only 5 notes, with one of the same note reused in the next octave above. With hundreds of millions of views online, *Oceans* has 7 notes in its entire song, with 2 of the same notes reused in the next octave above. The song *I'll Find You* by Lecrae uses 6 notes in the chorus in one octave, even though the featuring singer is a very capable vocalist. Both *Amazing Grace* and *Ocean*s have been translated into multiple languages for millions of listeners.

What Chords Communicate

I have a confession to make: I don't read music. Music theory bored me half to death when I was in school; it took the fun out of music for me. However, I play five instruments, and I also sing. You may be asking yourself, "How is that possible? Is he a freak of nature?" The answer is no; I am not. I'm not that special in that regard; many famous musicians do not read music. This is good news for you if you can't read music notation or chord charts very well. Those who do not read music taught themselves to play by feel and by ear. This may sound complicated at first, but it isn't, because music has predictable patterns and repetition that can be memorised. Over time you will be able to hear what chords are communicating and write lyrics appropriate to the feel of the music.

Chord Type	Associated Emotions
Major (e.g., C Major)	Happiness, cheerfulness, confidence, brightness, satisfaction, positive, strong, release
Minor (e.g., C minor)	Sadness, lement, reflective, longing, intensly energetic
Seventh (e.g., C7)	Funkiness, soulful, slightly edgy, tension
Major Seventh (e.g., CM7)	Love, serenity, tranquillity, exhilaration, floaty
Minor Seventh (e.g., Cm7)	Mellowness, beautiful, dreamy, subtle tension
Diminished (e.g., C°)	Clash, fear, shock, discomfort, unpleasant tension
Suspended Fourth (e.g., Csus4)	Delightful tension, anticipation, unresolved tension
Seventh, Minor Ninth (e.g., C7♭9)	Creepy, ominousness, dark
Added Ninth (e. g., Cadd9)	Nostalgia, openess, austerity

What chords communicate

When writing lyrics, remember that major chords communicate a strong expectation to the listener that something optimistic or "happy" is coming. In contrast, creating melody using minor chords communicates a feeling of "sadness," "bittersweet," and/or a feeling of "longing." Major 7 chords sound "pretty" and can communicate things such as the beauty of resting in God's presence, whereas diminished chords create a feeling of collision. Augmented and suspended chords convey tension and suspense as a "set up" of something else to follow. Your song will pack more of a punch when your melody, chord progression and lyrics work as one to deliver your message. Below is a simple table of chord types and their associated emotions that you can use as a guideline when writing lyrics. Remember that chords don't exist in isolation, so the associated emotions of a chord may change in context to the chord progression that you use.

Melody Making Framework

If you play an instrument, there are major and minor chord progressions in the back of this book to help spark melody ideas. Use the chord progressions and this simple framework to help you create melodies. Here are the steps to follow:

1. Use your phone's audio or video recorder to record the ideas you're about to make up.

2. Pick 3 chord progression in the back of this book and play them on your instrument.

3. Experiment with playing in different tempos and time signatures, and then choose the tempo/time signature/key combination that inspires you most.

4. Create 3 short melodies by humming over your 3 chord progressions. Make your melodies simple, between 5 to 7 notes, and each melody idea should be 10 to 30 seconds long.

5. Playback your three short melodies from your phone. Choose one melody that sounds to you most like a chorus, a different one that sounds most like a verse, and another that sounds most like a bridge.

6. Refine and improve these melodies as you write your lyrics.

7. If needed, add extra notes to your melodies. Try singing the melodies an octave above and an octave below for variety.

Tip: Your melodies may change and develop as you write. Remember to save old and new versions on your phone as a reference.

This framework will work for you no matter what genre you write. Some music purists might wrinkle their nose at this "basic" melody making framework, but after using it countless times with different clients in and out of the studio, I know it works, so use it. Later in chapter eight, you will learn a few simple steps so that your new awesome melodies can be played and appreciated even by music purists.

If your melodies feel "wonky" and awkward, especially at the beginning, that's okay. Just keep developing your melody ideas until they transform from something formless to taking shape. If you start to feel embarrassed at this stage in your collaboration that's also okay, you're probably taking yourself too seriously, relax. You're using your imagination and making things up in real-time, it's called "playing music", so keep playing. Your formless half idea could be the spark that triggers the full idea into ear-catching melodies.

Consider this; when describing his creative process, here's what Mozart, the world-famous and influential composer from the classic period observed, "Those ideas that please me I retain in memory and am accustomed, as I have been told, to hum them to myself. If I continue in this way, it soon occurs to me how I may turn this or that morsel to account so as to make a good dish of it. All this fires my soul". He's basically saying that he creates melodies the same way I'm saying you should, only he's saying it much better. Mozart said those words in the mid seventeen hundreds. That "basic" method of melody creation still works today.

If You Don't Play an Instrument

If you don't play an instrument, step 2 and step 3 of the melody making framework won't apply to you. However, you can still get access to great music quickly to help you create melodies using steps 1 and step 4 to 7. Just type the following search terms into YouTube to find music/chord progressions:

- "Chord progression in..." (A - G)
- "Free Instrumental..." (Guitar/Piano)
- "Free Instrumental..." (Pop/Rock/HipHop)

These search terms will bring back video results of ready-to-use recorded music either **by key, by instrument** or **by music genre** that are between 3 and 5 minutes long and to which you can write your lyrics. For even more options, type the same search terms in a search engine like Google to hear instrumentals from other websites. Some of the makers of these instrumentals will let you have them for free, and others will let you purchase them to record and release, helping you to avoid copyright issues later on. However, understand that if you choose this free or purchase option, you and 99 other people may have purchased that same instrumental to record with, so there will be other versions (both sacred and secular) out there.

I recommend that you use the instrumental **only** as inspiration to write lyrics and create a melody (without getting too attached to the instrumental itself). If you choose to record your song, use the chord progression in the instrumental as a reference so that your song sounds different from the idea that inspired it. A good music producer can create for you an original recording based on any song that inspired it, giving you a song that is uniquely yours without 99 other versions out there.

Finding Your Voice

Clients at the studio often talk to me about struggling to find their "voice." If you're also experiencing this, remember that it's a normal part of developing as a songwriter and musician, so don't be discouraged. I define having a voice in three ways: 1) having a "musical voice" which is the musicality, instrumentation, groove and energy of how you sound when performing live or on a recording, 2) having a "lyrical voice" which is the conviction of your message and what you often speak about that resonates with your listeners and 3) the tonal quality of your actual singing or rapping voice (i.e. pitch, timbre, cadence) that makes you sound unique. These three "voices" work together to make you sound like you. It may take writing or recording 30 to 70 songs to explore, discover and create as your voice develops .

Having a voice is the reason why you can hear songs for the first time by artists like Kirk Franklin, Toby Mac, Hillsong, and Tasha Cobbs and know that it's them because they've developed an authentic musical, lyrical and actual voice.

My experience from recording hundreds of musicians has shown that if you're struggling to find your voice, it helps to write more songs and build a large enough body of work — and that's what I recommend you do. When you have a large enough body of music (30 songs or more), you'll be able to analyse it all. More than likely a pattern will emerge that reveals a certain music vibe, what you typically write about, who you write for, your most-listened-to song, and your failures of trying to sound like someone else (which is okay for a small season but should be left behind with each song you write). All these things come together to help you find your voice, which you will uncover by just writing more songs.

The more you write songs, the more that melody and lyric creation will develop into an intuitive process for you. Your music will start to sound more genuine and more uniquely like you — and people want to hear your authenticity more than they want to listen to you do a lesser job of sounding like someone else. Those who are reading this book and have reached this milestone will agree with me, and those who haven't yet developed this intuition may be perplexed by what I mean. My advice to you is to keep writing and keep improving. I am excited for you to reach that milestone.

MAJOR BUILDING BLOCKS

Creating a song is like playing with Lego building blocks. You need both big blocks and small blocks in the right sequence to build a strong structure that many people can play with and not have it break. In the same way, songwriters also use big blocks and small blocks as well as sequences to build strong songs. Musicians need to be able to play instruments while people sing your song without it falling apart. This part of the book will cover music building blocks and how to build and sequence them so that your song is solid.

Simplicity is your friend when it comes to songwriting, so to simplify, there are **3 Major Building Blocks**, **5 Minor Building Blocks,** a **Song Title** and a **Hook** that can be used in creative combinations to build your song. You can increase or decrease the duration of any block to help deliver your song's message without being too wordy. It's worth noting that the names of these building blocks are different in different countries, which can create some confusion but rest assured, **they all do the same thing.** If you know them by a different name, use your best judgement and rename them in your mind to what you call them locally, or when collaborating with people from other countries.

Major Building Blocks

The three major building blocks include:

1. Verse

The verse is where you set the stage to deliver your song's message. It's your opportunity to build up details that tell a story, offer important information or provide more explanation in context before the chorus arrives. So if your song were a story, the verse would be the meat of it, a place where you list specific detail either literally or through metaphors. You get **full** creative license to paint a picture with words and **full** permission to describe the premise of your song using language that is biblical, truthful, imaginative, God-centred, emotive, engaging, and relevant. In the verses, you can go over background information that creates anticipation, tension, suspense, and excitement. You can also detail experiences, miracles, key characters, God, history or events that act as a vehicle to drive your song's key message forward.

Verses 1 and 2 usually have different lyrics because verse 2 typically continues where verse 1 ended and builds more detail while also creating a second setup for the chorus to soar again. The melody in verse 1 and verse 2 typically stays the same, which helps to make your song easier to remember for the listener. However, some small deviation from the original melody can be inserted into verse 2 to add a little variety. Adding some variety to the melody in verse 2 helps to interrupt the pattern and keep the listener's attention engaged, especially with longer songs. One very effective writing technique is to have a gradually ascending melody line with escalating lyrical *tension* at the same time, which seamlessly builds into the *release* of your chorus.

To make your song simpler and increase the chances of it being remembered, you can choose to have one verse that repeats lyrically and melodically in verse 1 and verse 2. However, avoid a third repetition unless it's a song for young children.

The first verse usually establishes several patterns at the same time like the time signature, the tempo of the song, syllables, rhyme scheme, and language. Once established, these patterns generally continue for the rest of your song. Rhyming may or may not be used in the verses, but when you create a rhyme scheme, it is best to repeat that rhyme scheme in the verses. I recommend you search YouTube and listen to some well-written verses; some examples are the songs *So Will I* by Hillsong, *This Is A Move* by Tasha Cobbs, and *Reckless Love* by Cory Asbury.

2. Chorus

The word chorus comes from the Greek word *Khoros*, which means a group of people singing the same thing at the same time. That's the result your chorus should achieve.

The chorus is where you place the key message of your song and is the part that people will remember most, hum, sing and whistle, so make it enjoyable. If you followed my previous instructions when writing your verse, you would have created a melody that gradually ascends throughout the verse with anticipation caused by layers of detail that you delivered using language that's engaging for the listener. These techniques used at the same time will escalate the **tension** in your verse and create an ideal situation for your chorus to arrive. Your chorus should contrast your verse and **release** that tension while simultaneously delivering the key message of your song.

To minimise being misunderstood, you must create a well-written chorus that can be sung and understood as a standalone piece. If someone were to read **only** the lyrics of your chorus and no other part of your song, they would understand your chorus as a self-contained message. A well-written chorus (or song title) is your song's key message that increases listener understanding and decreases confusion. Another chorus songwriting technique you must use for added impact is to make the melody and rhyme scheme in your chorus significantly different from your verse. The change of melody and rhyme scheme signals to listeners that it's a new section in the song.

To prevent your chorus from sounding dull and flat, change up the rhythm, lyrics, harmony and dynamics. It's also good to add the title of your song in the chorus because it increases the chances that people will remember your lyrics. What helps your chorus to stay in the mind of your listeners is one or more repetitions. So make your chorus more musically and emotionally engaging than other major blocks to make those repetitions enjoyable. Whenever you have three repeating choruses in your song, each one can rise in intensity a little more than the one before to keep the ears engaged. For this reason, the third chorus tends to be one of two places in your song where the intensity of the song reaches its maximum.

Part of the fun of songwriting is exploring what combination of these writing techniques will work best for the biblical message, emotional tone, musical groove and language for intended listeners of your song. One of the cardinal rules of songwriting is that your chorus **must** be heard at the 60-second mark or before. Otherwise, you risk losing listeners who aren't yet familiar with your music, and who'll press the skip button out of boredom. This rule is even more valid if you want your song to enter the charts or win awards. Later in chapter 8, you will learn more about the four critical times in your song and what you must do at those times.

3. Bridge

The bridge (some countries call this the "middle eight"), adds a sense of progress to your song. It's generally placed after the second chorus either before or after an instrumental. The bridge is an opportunity for you to add information that wasn't previously mentioned, to clarify any lyrical loose ends, or to create contrast. In the bridge you get an opportunity to add to, or entirely change the mood, melody or chord progression that came before.

A bridge can be a "boredom-breaker" to lessen the listener's fatigue from elements that repeat in your song, so it must create a noticeable shift, but still complement the message of your song. The bridge is the second most natural place to put the lyrical, emotional and musical climax or anticlimax of your song. If you put the emotional peak of your song in the bridge, the chorus after the bridge could be a down-chorus, whereas if the emotional peak is placed in the third chorus, you could have a down-bridge for contrast. This way, they won't compete as the peak of your song unless you want to sustain the emotional intensity and have two peaks on purpose. Although the bridge is a major building block, not all songs need a bridge, and this topic will be covered more in chapter 5 when you learn about the seven songs structures.

A songwriting technique you can use to write your bridge is to use the word **but** to introduce contrast with what came before. The word **but** also comes in different forms such as **still, even so, yet, however, although and just the same**. Another writing technique that will help you produce contrast is to explore or answer the question **what if** and making that your bridge. It offers a different side of the story in an interesting way. Lastly, you can simply summarise your verses and choruses for the listener using different words and make that your bridge.

Missing Information

Between the verses, chorus, and bridge, you should have established the premise of your song, explained any detail, and clarified any points that would otherwise confuse first-time listeners. All of this should be engaging for your listeners and take them to your song's key message, which is often in your chorus or song title.

Anytime you have unexplained detail, it creates unanswered questions in the minds of your listeners, which is bad if you didn't mean to do so. The unanswered questions can become points of "friction" that makes it harder for your listeners to connect with your song and to God. Some listeners can become so fixated with "figuring out" the answer that they miss your message entirely. Where there's no answer available, the imagination of your listeners will fill the gap that your lyrics created with a meaning you didn't intend.

Avoid Being Ignored

As a songwriter, you should take into account that human ears have a strong tendency to ignore repetitive, predictable and ongoing sounds (such as a chorus), and focus instead on new and novel sounds. That's the reason why your ears can ignore the sound of your car engine running as you drive but will notice new sounds, signalling to you that it's time to fix something.

That same human tendency to ignore the familiar is activated if your song repeats the same lyrics and melody too many times; the ears tune out a little (or a lot). So how can you address this pesky little problem in your songwriting so that listeners engage for longer? The answer is to **repeat yourself skillfully** by adding layers of lyrical or musical detail (See adlibs in the next section). If you have a third or fourth chorus, consider using adlibs or alternate lyrics that make it just a little different and interesting with each repetition.

An excellent example of skilful repetition is the song *What A Beautiful Name* by Hillsong. Although the chorus repeats three times, there's one word different in each chorus: "beautiful," "wonderful," and “powerful." And even though there's a double bridge in that song, one is arranged as a breakdown bridge and the other with full instrumentation to give you a sonic difference to something already familiar.

MINOR BUILDING BLOCKS

Now that you know about the three major building blocks, you will be able to make much easier sense of the minor building blocks. But before you learn about the minor building blocks, it's first useful to cover the song title and the hook.

Song Title

Your song title plays a vital role because the very first interaction a person will have with your song is either hearing your song title recommended by a friend, reading your song title just before pressing play or asking someone "what song is this?". The purpose of your song title is to help listeners quickly identify your song by name, tell or hint to listeners what your song is about and pique their interest and curiosity enough so that they want to press play. Imagine yourself as the ideal listener searching for your song, would your song title attract and stay with him or her?

There is an ocean of music online, and your song title should act as a beacon of light attracting your ideal listener. So do your best to give your songs titles that are easy to remember, impossible to forget and makes listeners want to press the play button. Your song title should:

- Be just 1 song title (avoid 2; this creates confusion)
- Be 5 words long or less (but longer than just 1 word)
- Ideally, the same as your "hook"/the last line in your chorus
- Be relevant to your target listeners
- Avoid words that can be misinterpreted (even if they're relevant)
- Contain alliteration or rhyme (if possible)

- Match your message (Don't title your song *Fasting* if the message is God's love. *Your Love* is a better match)

It is not possible for every song title you create to meet all these requirements and that's okay. The idea is to include whenever possible as many of these points as your song title will allow because it increases the likelihood of being easy to remember and difficult to forget.

One approach that could help is to create your song title first and then write your song. That way, you can include as many of the above points as possible. It focuses your lyrics and allows you to insert your title in the most memorable places where titles get remembered. Other places where your song title could come from may be:

1. The first line of verse 1
2. The last line of verse 1
3. A memorable line in your bridge

Choosing your song title from these three places is less common and is not something I recommend. It may confuse your listeners, who will probably give your song an alternate title (usually from the chorus) that they think your song ought to be called, and sometimes their title will stick better than yours.

Hook

The **hook** and the song title are practically the same thing in modern songwriting techniques. However, there are multiple kinds of hooks and it just so happens that the title hook is the most popular. So what is a hook? A hook is anything catchy or memorable in your song that metaphorically hooks a listener's ear and makes them want to hear more. There are four kinds of hooks in a song:

1. Song title hook
2. Lyrical hook
3. Instrumental hook (A repeating riff)
4. Production hook (In recorded music, this hook gets added by a music producer, and it can be a non-melodic and a non-lyrical sound)

Depending on what genre you write, hooks may have more or less importance in your song, so you may or may not need one. Some examples of song title hooks are Chris Tomlin who details all the goodness of God in his verses, which nicely sets up the title hook to conclude *How Great Is Our God.* Todd Dulaney's title hook arrives after he details in his verse about how something happens that we cannot explain when we call on *Your Great Name.* Tasha Cobbs describes in her verse miracles that God is still doing, which leads her to proclaim her title hook *This Is A Move* in the chorus. The best place to put title hooks include:

1. The last line in your chorus (Prime real estate for song titles)
2. The first line of the chorus (Second place for song titles)
3. The whole chorus is a hook (*This Is A Move* by Tasha Cobbs)

Titling your song based on the hook is a powerful songwriting technique that you should use because if someone (who's never heard of you) hears your song for the first time, they should know the title at the one-minute mark. When you strategically place your title hook in the first or last line of the chorus, you increase the chances of your song being remembered and discovered.

Lyrical hooks are different from title hooks. Title hooks can be found in the chorus, whereas lyrical hooks can be found elsewhere, such as in the verses or the bridge. Sometimes well-written lyrics in the verses or bridge can outshine your song title, which is one of the reasons why songs sometimes develop two song titles. Examples of lyrical hooks include songs such as *Here I Am To Worship* by Tim Hughes, which is often referred to by its lyrical hook, "Light of The World," the opening line in verse one. Matt Redman's song, *Heart of Worship,* is best known as "When The Music Fades," also a lyrical hook in the opening line of verse one. I don't believe the writers intentionally mean to create two song titles; it's just a byproduct of good songwriting that resonates with listeners.

Instrumental and production hooks are simple and self-explanatory enough. They were explained in brief earlier, and because this book is short and focuses on writing lyrics, they won't be covered in depth. Just know that when you stack hooks into one song, you massively increase its catchiness. But you also risk the "annoying" factor, so be careful not to overdo it.

Now, let's get back to the five minor building blocks. They help you to seamlessly transition your lyrics and melody when going **into** or coming **out of** any major building block. The five minor building blocks are:

1. Intro

As the name suggests, the introduction happens at the beginning of the song. It can be used to establish one or more expectations of what's to come, such as mood, key, tempo, time signature, instrumentation, melody, vocals and more. An intro can be one or more bars in length and can add a sense of suspense and anticipation that is released once the song transitions into vocal performance. Although less common, some songs don't have an introduction by choice and instead start straight into verse one; an intro is optional and flexible.

2. Pre-Chorus / Rise / Climb / Lift

The Pre-Chorus acts like a link that connects the verse to the chorus. It goes by different names because it achieves several things at the same time. A Pre-Chorus can raise the melody, ramp up the rhythm, and lift the intensity of the harmonies while preparing the way for your chorus. An example can be heard in the song *You Are Good* by Israel Houghton. Notice how the two lines of his Pre-Chorus are different in melody, rhyme and intensity to the verse and how the song's energy shifts momentarily in the Pre-Chorus, linking seamlessly into the chorus that soars. A second Pre-Chorus example is *I'll Find You* by Lecrae, which changes the song melodically and rhythmically and escalates the song only to suddenly drop into a Down-chorus. Building musical intensity in the Pre-Chorus and then dropping the intensity in this way creates an anti-climactic effect that makes your listeners focus on the lyrics of your chorus even more than usual.

In short, a Pre-Chorus is used to change the rhyme scheme, melody and rhythm of your song. It can also be two, four or six lines long, which creates tension by implying or actually using the words "if," "maybe," "and," "but," "when" or "why." When used well, the Pre-Chorus is an effective tool for your songwriting.

3. Refrain

The refrain is one or two lines that get repeated from verse to verse. Please don't confuse a refrain with the chorus because a refrain is not a major building block; it is fundamentally a part of the verse and is usually, but not always, written as the last line in the verse. It can act as a lyrical hook of a song, and sometimes the refrain can also be the song title. You can hear two examples of a refrain in the songs *What a Friend We Have in Jesus*, which ends every verse with the refrain "Everything to God in Prayer" and an alternate refrain of "Take it to the Lord in Prayer." A second example of a refrain can be heard in the song *Till I See You* by Hillsong United, which ends each verse with the refrain "I'll trust in you."

4. Interlude / Solo / Instrumental / Breakdown / Tag / Adlib

An interlude is a simple way to introduce a lyrical or instrumental section in your song. You may choose to add an instrumental interlude to allow singers to catch their breath before their next part, feature a solo, slow down or speed up your song's momentum, or introduce a key or metre change. Interludes can be short or long, lasting between 1 and 8 bars or maybe longer, depending on the needs of your song. Interludes are transitional by nature, so use one any time you need to transition from one part of your song to the other.

An adlib is simply a special kind of interlude that gets layered on top of other parts lasting 1 bar or longer. Adlibs are improvisational by nature, meaning that the singer/musician has full permission to create something on the spot not previously prepared. Lyrical adlibs can be vowel sounds such as "ooh", "ah" and "oh." They can also be words like "yeah," but be careful. It's easy to add "yeah" as a lyric, which can work in genres such as Hip Hop and Pop, but sounds like lazy writing in some Contemporary Christian songs and Hymns. In other words, understand the audience and understand the genre. Adlibs can also be the lead vocals being echoed or sung in "cannon" that reinforce your song's key message.

5. Outro

As suggested by the name, the purpose of an Outro is to transition your song out to finish. You may choose to end your song suddenly and abruptly, in which case you don't need an Outro. A different Outro is to fade out or remove one musical component at a time until the song's momentum dies down, leading it to end. An Outro is both optional and flexible, so you can get creative experimenting with a "perfect ending" or an "imperfect ending." Have fun with your outro and see which one best suits your song.

Honourable Mention

One honourable mention that could be considered both a major or a minor building block is the Post-Chorus. As the name suggests, it features after the chorus and can sometimes get confused as the chorus itself. In some genres the Post-chorus is fully instrumental; when this technique is used, a Post-chorus can sound like an interlude. However, in other genres, the Post-Chorus may have lyrics that can be a few lines or a few words that repeat; when this technique is used, the Post-chorus can make the actual chorus sound like a Pre-chorus. It's okay if that confused you a little, just read that paragraph again for clarity.

Writing a Post-chorus has been trending in and out of music over many years. There's no telling yet whether it's going to stay for good or trend out of popularity altogether. Until then you're welcome to use it creatively to meet the vision of your song.

Now that you know about minor building blocks, the hook, and how to create a song title, you are ready to move to the next step — the P.I.M.S method, which will show you how to translate what you are feeling into words for maximum impact.

THE P.I.M.S METHOD

Struggling To Find the Words?

Have you ever started writing a song and thought to yourself, "I don't know how to express what I am feeling" or "I don't know what words to use?" If so, the P.I.M.S Method is a songwriting approach I use that you can also apply to help translate your emotions into lyrics. But before I reveal what the P.I.M.S Method is, it is crucial to embrace one key mindset that will supercharge this writing technique in your favour even more.

Use Your Creative Licence

As a songwriter, you need to embrace the mindset of "Creative Licence," also known as the "Artistic Licence" mindset. This means that as the creator of a song, you have full permission from your listeners to communicate truthfully and tell a story — not at the level of everyday reality, but two or more levels above. You have the green light to exercise your creative freedom through your unique perspective that helps people to connect with God.

It's similar to when you watch an engaging, enjoyable film. The director uses his creative licence to increase the emotional impact in the story, so you connect with the characters; when you connect, the director did an excellent job of communicating visually. In the same way, you also have full permission from your listeners to communicate emotionally to them in a way that impacts spiritually and helps them to connect to God. You get to paint a picture with words, and the P.I.M.S Method is like your lyrical colour palette.

The P.I.M.S Method

P.I.M.S is an acronym that helps your lyrics to pack more of a punch. The acronym stands for **P**oetry, **I**magery, **M**etaphor and **S**imile, and it's so effective that you **don't** have to use all four in the same song; one or two used well will create the desired impact. Applying P.I.M.S will make your lyrics more layered, your experiences more relatable, portray imagery more clearly and also convey emotion. In short, using P.I.M.S delivers detailed and descriptive language that engages your listeners.

The concept of P.I.M.S works for all music styles; the only thing that changes is the use of language and slang that's specific to a genre. Although it's true that "there is nothing new under the sun" *(Eccl 1:9),* what will make your song unique is how **you** express it. Your unique experiences, your perspective, and the words you use will help people to connect with God easier than other songs. That's worth repeating: your songs will reach people for God that others cannot. So start reading your Bible daily so you can better know the word of God. Also, start paying attention to the language (words) of those who God put on your heart to reach through music.

Here are some definitions and examples to help you better understand and use the P.I.M.S Method:

Poetry is a piece of writing that blends the nature of regular speech and song at the same time. Poetry is nearly always rhythmical and uses formal layouts and elements like metre, rhyme and stanza in its structure. Poetry can be found in many hymns because many old hymns originally started out as poems and didn't get paired up with melodies until much later. One famous poem that was later made into a song is the poem *Amazing Grace* by John Newton, which can be translated into everyday language as follows: **"It's amazing to hear of a grace that gave a sinner like me salvation. I was a lost soul. I couldn't see it back then, but I see it now."** Instead, John Newton poetically wrote:

"Amazing grace, how sweet the sound
That saved a wretch like me.
I once was lost, but now I'm found
Was blind but now I see…"

Hundreds of years later, we are still singing that masterfully written poem. If everyday language just isn't "doing it" for your song, it might be the right time for you to get poetic.

Imagery is the use of vivid and descriptive language to add visual depth to your song. When you use sensory imagery, it appeals to human senses and helps your listeners relate to as well as understand your song's message. Imagery is most powerful when it engages one or more of the five senses of sight, hearing, smell, taste and touch. Doing so allows your listeners to "see" what you mean.

An example of imagery can be heard in the song *Oceans* by Hillsong, which makes excellent use of water imagery. Joel Houston and his co-writers could have written: **"You ask me to rely on you in turbulent times when my faith feels like it's walking on a faulty foundation."** Instead, through the use of imagery, they wrote:

"You call me out upon the waters, the great unknown where feet may fail..."

Those lyrics pack a visual punch and allow the listener to remember the Bible story of Jesus calling Peter off the boat and onto the water, and to rely on Him so Peter could also walk on water — the impossible made real through Christ. The song *Oceans* masterfully uses the imagery writing technique. You can apply the same method of imagery to paint a picture in the frame of your listeners' understanding. It will help to bridge the gap between their reality and the higher calling from God.

Metaphor is a figure of speech where a word or a phrase is used to represent or symbolise something else, especially something abstract. The Greek word for metaphor is *metapherein* which means to transfer. Metaphors provide clarity or identify hidden similarities between two ideas.

Metaphors can be heard everywhere in music. An example of a metaphor in full swing can be heard in the bridge of the song *Reckless Love* by Bethel Music. Cory Asbury and his co-writers could have boringly written, **"I'm the stupid sheep that drifted away, but your fierce love took the risk of total loss to come and find me."** Instead, the writers made full use of their artistic license and used the entire bridge as a metaphor for The Parable of the Lost Sheep saying:

> "...There's no wall you won't kick down, lie you won't tear down, coming after me..."

Use metaphors in your lyrics when symbolism is needed. It's an excellent way to teach listeners something they don't yet know about God by linking it to something similar in their personal reality. It will give them that "uh-huh, lightbulb moment."

I believe this is the reason why Jesus often taught in parables. Jesus told Peter and Andrew, two brothers who knew all about the reality of fishing professionally to "Come follow me, and I will send you out to fish for people" *(Matt 4:19)*. I believe the lightbulb switched on in their brain because they understood the symbolism in that metaphor to become fishers of men. It linked what they did daily to a higher calling for Jesus, and that's why "at once they left their nets and followed Him" *(Matt 4:20)*.

Simile is a different figure of speech which directly compares two **unlike** things. The word simile comes from the Latin word *similis* (meaning "similar, like"), so a simile will contain the words "as" or "like" (e.g. love **like** a father; brave **as** a lion).

An example of similes at work can be heard in verse 1 of the song *Ever Be* by Bethel Music. The songwriter Kalley Heiligenthal, could have written: **"Your love is dedicated; it stands the test of time, pre-**

dating Jacob's wrestle and you keep your word." Instead, through the use of similes, she wrote:

"Your love is devoted **like** a ring of solid gold, **like** a vow that is tested, **like** a covenant of old…"

Similes are different from metaphors. Although both get used for making comparisons, similes use the words **like** and **as** to compare things, such as "God's love is **like** an ocean." In contrast, metaphors directly **state** a comparison: "God's love is an ocean."

Use similes in your lyrics to make a comparison between two things that **seem** to have very little in common, yet convey a deeper message to the listener. Just like Jesus did, many times in the Bible when teaching people about heaven, Jesus would say: "The kingdom of heaven is **like…**" *(Matt 13:24, 31, 33, 44, 45, 47, 52).*

In summary, the P.I.M.S method is powerful for helping you find your lyrics and creating more emotional, spiritual and theological impact. What's even better is that you don't have to use all four approaches; one or two per song will create the desired result.

Beware!

A **warning** about the P.I.M.S Method and your creative licence: don't overdo it! Some songwriters take their lyrics too far and end up writing a song with almost no resemblance to the Bible because they overused this technique and include all four letters of the acronym in one song.

Their message gets drowned in pointless poetry, too many metaphors and blurry imagery, making the whole song too wishy-washy. In short, the song ends up with zero substance. It starts to resemble a film such as *The Lord of the Rings* instead of the Bible's truth of a good God who gives salvation to sinners like us. Be biblical; don't be bombastic.

Your song must have Godly, biblical and theological substance or it will crash and burn and for a good reason. The purpose of your song is to worship God and lead others to connect to Him, deliver a message or tell a story (testimony). If your song lacks substance, it will not achieve any of those goals. To avoid writing songs that are meaningless, read the Bible as a reference when writing songs; it has all the answers you need. If you're ever in doubt if your lyrics have gone too far, just keep it simple.

Your Predictable Problem

Confusion is a pesky little problem that will show up from time to time with listeners and that's okay. You can never completely remove confusion; you can only reduce how much and how frequently people get confused by your lyrics. Let's look at ways of minimising confusion, so your song is not misunderstood or misinterpreted.

Minimise Misunderstanding (The 4 Questions)

What I've learned over the years is that good communication can be tricky to achieve between people, so misunderstanding **is** the rule, **not** the exception. The majority of people do not communicate proactively and most people do not listen actively. As a result, people are highly likely to miss details and get confused because of bad or incomplete communication.

As a songwriter, you are the communicator, and it's your job to communicate through the medium of music as clearly as possible. You cannot control whether people are good listeners; you can only control communicating well in complete thoughts to minimise misunderstanding — and you can do this by assuming that there are faults in your lyric and question your song. The 4 questions to ask yourself about your lyrics are **what, how, why** and **what if.**

Here's an example of how the 4 questions can work for you. Imagine you write a song titled *God You're So Good*, and the lyrics in the chorus go like this:

> "God you're so good, you're so good, my lips will sing your praise, every single day because you're so good."

Now let's imagine that a listener tunes in to your song during the chorus and hears those lyrics. Let's also assume that your melody is good, so the listener feels invited in and feels compelled to listen longer. Using the four questions, you may choose to structure your song like this:

- The chorus could cover **what** your song is about
- Verse 1 could answer the question **why** God is so good
- Verse 2 could detail **how** God is good to you
- The bridge could explore the question: but **what if** no one ever told you about God's goodness, what would your life be?

As you can see from this example, the 4 questions are a pretty straightforward way to structure your song. When the lyrics in your song address all 4 questions, it drastically reduces the amount of confusion that people experience when listening to your song. If they don't get answered, it means you left something unexplained, which creates some "friction" for the listener. You may then need to rewrite a few lines.

How To Use the 4 Questions

You are allowed to reword the 4 questions to fit the topic of your song. What will change the question's wording is the context of your song and whether you ask the questions before or after you finish writing your lyrics. The point is to assume fault in your lyrics and ask the questions "why," "what," "how" and "what if." The answer to those questions should be somewhere in your lyrics, either explicitly or implicitly. If they are not, rewrite any confusing lines that need to be rewritten. Below is just one version of rewording the 4 questions as a starting point to help you understand the concept:

1. What's the biblical message of my song?
2. Why is it true?
3. How is it true for me?
4. What if I didn't know this truth?

The 4 questions are too versatile and songwriting is too dynamic to list endless examples. Simply repurpose them for your writing and make sure your lyrics address as many as needed to help minimise confusion for listeners.

The purpose of the P.I.M.S method, the four questions and all the techniques you've learned so far is to become so skilled with words that people GET IT, to sharpen your talent with language that people FEEL IT and to describe things in such a way that people SEE IT. This is a fun challenge; this is your challenge, so rise to the occasion.

RHYMING

Many people know what rhyming is and can even give an example. However, fewer people know what a rhyme scheme is. For clarification, a rhyme scheme is a pattern of rhyming that is created when you rhyme words at the end of a line of lyric. These are called "end rhymes." When you create multiple end rhymes over multiple lines, you establish a rhyming pattern, also known as a rhyme scheme. The next page shows a simple example of end rhymes that create a rhyme scheme pattern from the song *Do*

Verse 1	**Rhyme Scheme**
Walking around these **walls**	A
I thought by now they'd **fall**	A
But You have never failed me **yet**	B
Waiting for change to **come**	C
Knowing the battle's **won**	C *(half rhyme)*
For You have never failed me **yet**	B
Chorus	
Your promise still **stands**	A
Great is Your faithfulness, **faithfulness**	B
I'm still in Your **hands**	A
This is my confidence, You've never failed me **yet**	C

How to create a rhyme scheme

It Again by Elevation Worship.

When it comes to rhyme schemes, the rule of thumb is that your rhyme scheme pattern must change in the verse, chorus and bridge. For example, your rhyme scheme in verse 1 and verse 2 can follow the same pattern because they're both verses. However, the rhyme scheme in your chorus should be different from the verse, which should be different from the bridge. Having different rhyme schemes signals to your listeners that this is a different part of the song, and it makes your song easier to remember.

Notice how the rhyme scheme pattern changes from AABCCB in the verse to an ABABC pattern in the chorus, and later it changes to an AABA pattern in the bridge. Additionally, in this song, we see the use of a half-rhyme, which you can also apply in your songwriting. A half-rhyme, also known as an "imperfect rhyme," involves using two words that are not an exact rhyme, but sound close enough to each other to be used as near rhyming words. For example, the words "heart" and "apart" are perfect rhymes, but the words "ocean" and "open" are half-rhymes.

Your rhyme scheme can follow any pattern you establish. However, make sure the pattern remains consistent for that building block once it is created. Also, if your title hook is the last line of your chorus (a very important placement) as it often should be, avoid rhyming your title hook with other words in your chorus. That way, your title hook will stand out and be remembered even more.

Lastly, you can also make use of internal rhyme schemes. As the name suggests, internal rhymes are words positioned in the middle of one or multiple lines of lyric. An example of internal rhymes combined with half-rhymes can be heard in the song Your Great Name by Todd Dulaney.

Verse	**Rhyme Scheme**
We love to call your **name,** it's something, we cannot **explain**	A
That happens, when we **proclaim** your great name, your great **name**	B

How to create an internal rhyme scheme

In a nutshell, that's all you need to know to master rhyming and rhyme schemes in your songwriting. You can use perfect (full), and imperfect (half) rhymes, as well as internal and end rhyme schemes in creative combinations to make your songs easy for listeners to remember and sing along with. Practice makes permanent.

KEY POINTS FROM HOW TO WRITE LYRICS PART 1

Melody Is Important

Melody is attractive to the human ear; it invites someone to listen longer. Keep your melodies simple; 5 to 7 notes are enough of an "invitation." For young children, try writing an easier 4-note melody.

Your Melody Must Change

Your verse, chorus, pre-chorus and bridge must have different melodies. If not, you risk sounding monotonous and boring. People will tune out.

Your Melody Has a Mood

Your melody is already communicating something without lyrics. Good melody complements the lyrics like a hand in a fitted glove.

You Have 10 Parameters To Play With When Songwriting

There are 3 major building blocks, 5 minor building blocks, a hook and a song title available to you. Each block makes room for you to get lyrically and musically creative in a way that's relevant to your target listener.

Repeat Yourself Masterfully

Human ears can tune out. If repeating yourself for the third and fourth time, add some engaging musical or lyrical detail not previously heard.

Use the P.I.M.S Method To Translate Emotions Into Words

Poetry, Imagery, Metaphors and Similes are tools to help your lyrics pack an emotional punch. The P.I.M.S method lets you use original language that connects with people and paints a complete image of how you feel.

Misunderstanding Is the Rule, Not the Exception

Remember that people are not in your head and won't automatically understand what you mean. If you feel your lyrics may confuse listeners, clarify them by using one or more of the 4 Questions either after you finish writing your song or use them as you're writing.

Rhymes Get Remembered

After your melody, people remember your rhyme scheme, especially end rhymes. Use the same rhyme scheme pattern in your verses, use a different pattern in the chorus, and change it again in the bridge; this is essential. Avoid rhyming your title hook with other parts in your song.

CHAPTER 4
HOW TO WRITE LYRICS PART 2

HOW TO USE SYLLABLES

Have you ever found yourself singing a song and later noticing that you knew a lot more of the lyrics than you realised? How does that happen? One reason why those lyrics are almost impossible to forget is because the writer has used as many words as possible that only have one syllable. What is a syllable? A syllable is a single unbroken sound of a spoken or written word. For example, the word:

- God has 1 syllable **God**
- Answer has 2 syllables **An**-swer
- Responding has 3 syllables **Res**-pon-**ding**
- Holy Spirit has 4 syllables **Ho**-ly **Spi**-rit
- Phenomenally has 5 syllables **Phe**-nom-**e**-nal-**ly**

What I do, that you may also find useful, is to count with my fingers as I say each syllable. For whatever reason, my studio clients are more receptive to rewriting lyrics when they can hear each syllable as well as see it counted on my hand. Use this songwriting hack when showing your collaborator that he or she has too many or too few syllables in a certain line.

A general guideline to follow is the more syllables that you use in one word, the more you risk confusing people; in other words, a lot of people struggle to understand long words. Below are some examples of multiple syllables (long words) compared to fewer syllables (short words). As you read these examples, notice how your brain has to work just a little harder to understand longer words with more syllables:

- It's **uncomplicated** vs It's **simple (5 syllables vs 2)**
- He was **devastated** vs He was **sad (4 syllables vs 1)**
- I was so **abrupt** vs I was so **blunt (2 syllables vs 1)**

Did you notice your brain working just a smidge harder to recognise and understand longer words? Did you also notice how your brain breezed by short words without much effort? That's because single-syllable words are more comfortable to recognise, understand, sing and remember. In other words, don't use $5 words when $1 words will do. I'm not saying you should dumb it down and never use big words; I'm just highlighting the "mental friction" created when you overcomplicate lyrics. If you create too much friction in one song, people will tune out because you're making it harder for them than it should be, people should not have to reach for the dictionary. Finding the right words is a fun challenge of songwriting that you should welcome.

As a music producer, I often have five goals when I am recording my clients in the studio:

1. Create a song that glorifies God
2. Create a song that my client loves
3. Create the "Ooh Factor," which is when someone says "Ooh, play it again"

4. Create a song that listeners like, remember and can sing after hearing it 1 to 7 times
5. Create a song that a non-English speaker can sing (even just a little bit) after hearing it a few times

The best way to achieve these five goals is by writing a great song peppered with as many single-syllable words as possible. Use the same five goals in your songwriting to create songs that connect with listeners.

Longer words with multiple syllables do have the advantage of sounding quite rhythmic and can be the perfect fit for what you want to say. You may also need fewer lyrics when words have more syllables, but I still subscribe to the idea that less is more. Use words economically; it's worth it to make a big impact with small words, to be effective and efficient, to say the most, but speak the least when delivering God's message. The challenge of changing your perspective in several ways until you find words that fit gives you a rewarding feeling. I'm positive you'll grow to love it, too.

Writing Hymns

If your goal is to write hymns, you will also need to count syllables in each **line** of lyrics. This will help you to keep within the writing pattern and poetic style of hymnal songs. The next page shows syllables per line in action in the hymn *Amazing Grace* so that you better understand the concept of syllables (or "accents") per line.

Hymns are simply poems set to music. Because they're poems, they get written a little differently than modern Christian songs. Your hymn lyrics will need to be written in fixed "metrical patterns," meaning a fixed number of syllables and accents per line of lyrics. I recommend that you use the three most common metrical patterns to write your hymns:

Verse 1	**Syllables / Accents**
Amazing Grace, How sweet the sound	8
That saved a wretch like me	6
I once was lost, but now am found	8
T'was blind but now I see	6
Verse 2	
T'was Grace that taught my heart to fear	8
And Grace, my fears relieved	6
How precious did that grace appear	8
The hour I first believed	6

How to structure syllables & accents in hymns

1. Long metre: All lyric lines are eight syllables long — for example **(88.88)** like in the hymn *In Christ Alone.*

2. Common metre: Alternating eight and six syllables per lyric line — for example **(86.86)** like in the hymn *Amazing Grace.*

3. Short metre: The 1st, 2nd and 4th lyric lines are six syllables per line while the 3rd lyric line is eight syllables long — for example **(66.86)** like in the hymn *Crown Him With Many Crowns.*

What makes hymns sound like hymns is the use of fixed metrical patterns (syllables and accents) and the use of poetic language. I suggest listening to all three of those hymns if you've never heard them before and count the syllables per line so that you understand metrical patterns a little better. Also, refer back to the "P" in the P.I.M.S method to help you when writing your next hymn.

These hymns were written hundreds of years ago and are still being sung today. *Amazing Grace*, for example, was written in the year 1772 and has been covered in multiple languages by many local and international musicians. As a fun exercise, search the words "Amazing Grace in…" on YouTube or Google and count for yourself how many languages predictive text generates for you. Spoiler alert: there are a lot. This is an example of how long a well-written and meaningful song can live when given some thought.

Now you know that single-syllable words are crucial for helping people to remember your lyrics, as well as making your songs more singable.

Next, you need to figure out what types of songs you are writing. Do you know which types of songs work well with certain listeners and which songs don't? Is there a framework for writing lyrics to help those listeners? You need to know this if you want to connect with your ideal listener in a powerful way. Keep reading to learn the answers to these questions and more.

THE 5 CATEGORY OF CHRISTIAN SONGS

What types of songs are you writing? Do you even know? Are they relevant? Are they the types of lyrics that make people think about God, smile, laugh, cry or dance? Is there a way to laser focus your song to create that kind of impact? Yes, there is! The answer is: don't write a song for "everyone" or for "every occasion." Nothing says **beginner** or **inexperienced** more than trying to write songs for "everyone."

If your goal is to make everyone happy or make them like you through songwriting, stop reading this book right now because that will never happen. If that last statement created a mini-earthquake in your brain, be happy, because that's the sound of your false belief breaking (as it should). Not everyone will like your songs, and that's okay.

Here's a more practical approach to genuinely help people worship God through your music ministry. Yes, when you write songs that glorify God and help others do the same, you are participating in music ministry. Back to that practical approach; instead of **broadcasting** by trying to write songs for everyone and every occasion, a better way to write songs is **narrowcasting**, which means writing lyrics that focus on certain people and certain situations. Your song is less likely to connect and succeed when your lyrics are too general. The opposite is also true; when your lyrics are focused, your song stands a better chance of connecting and succeeding. So give your song focus by narrowcasting.

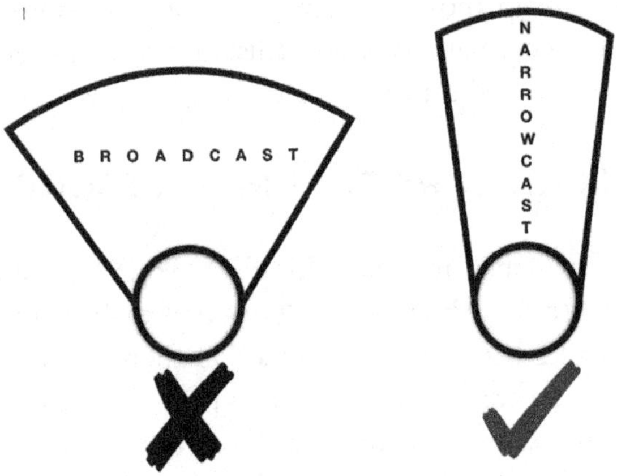

Broadcast lyrics vs Narrowcast lyrics

Although there are many Christian songs out there, God gave me a revelation one morning at 4 a.m. that they all fall into one of five categories or a combination. So what are these five categories?

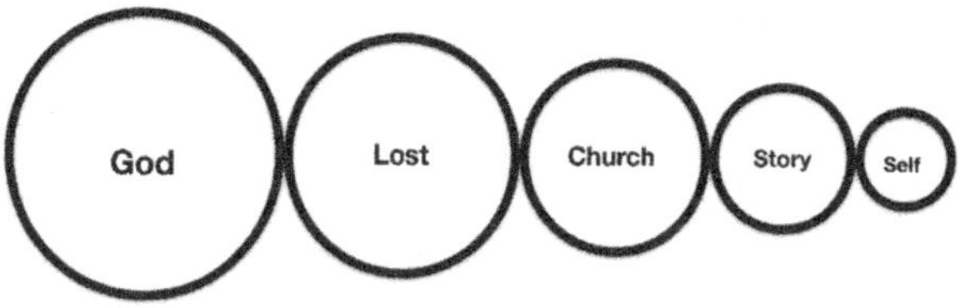

The 5 categories of Christian songs

1. God Song

God songs are the first and most important category of Christian songs. Why? As Christians, God should be our number one priority, and we are to praise and worship Him as the Bible instructs us to as believers. Whether you're a first-time writer or a seasoned professional, your first or next song should be to write a God Song. God songs are written to describe God and to ascribe worship to Him as you learned in chapter one. God songs do the following:

- Praise and worship God
- Speak about His nature, character and goodness

(Hint: find this in your Bible and your testimony)

- Invites God the Father, Son and Holy Spirit
- Give thanks to God for the countless things he does
- Ask for help; make your requests known to God
- Speak of miracles and wonders He is doing or has done
- Echos the word of God as in the Bible

That list is not comprehensive or exhaustive. There are many ways to write a God Song; the main thing is that your God song focuses on speaking to God and about God. One small tell-tale sign that your spiritual maturity is improving is that you'll transition from talking about God (praise) to talking with and to God, giving Him all credit (worship). Worship entails knowing God more intimately, and some of your most meaningful songs will come from your worship.

In the first chapter, you learned about putting God into your song explicitly and implicitly. Although implicitly adding God (Him, You, He) can work in this category, I believe God Songs work best when you **explicitly** put **God, Jesus, Holy Spirit, Lord, King** or the other Hebrew names of God or the English equivalent into your lyrics. This makes it clear who your song is about; there's no guesswork. When you're writing a God Song that is intimate and expresses how much you love and adore Him, there are two things you should do: 1) use the name of God explicitly, and 2) be more selective with your language so you avoid sounding like a romance novel or a Billboard Top 40 Pop love song. If you ignore those two steps, your lyrics of love may distract people during solemn times of worship. Although it's impossible to make everyone happy, your God Song is for an audience of one — Him. So use these simple songwriting steps to please Him by writing a biblically-based song of praise, thanksgiving and worship that also leads others to worship. So what can you write about that God has done for or around you?

2. Lost Song

Lost Songs are the second category of Christian songs that focus on reaching people with no knowledge of or faith in God. These songs reach people who haven't yet accepted Jesus Christ as their Lord and Saviour; they also reach those who used to have faith but have lost it. When you write a Lost Song, you are fulfilling a part of the Great Commission *(Matt 28:18-20),* which is to make disciples of all nations, teaching people to obey Jesus' commands and to be baptised in the name of the Father, Son and Holy Spirit.

You can put God into your Lost Song implicitly or explicitly, depending on the audience. Some Christians use the phrase "seeker-sensitive" as though it's a bad thing when describing certain songs; in this context, it is not a bad thing at all. As the songwriter, you have to be sensitive to what the seeker needs most. Your lyrics should then do the work of acknowledging those needs and connecting them to Christ. Otherwise, you will point them in the wrong direction.

When writing Lost Song lyrics, you can expect to blend language from the world of that listener (without profanity) with the Bible's truth to bridge the gap. Using heavy theology, fire and brimstone, New King James English will not connect with this kind of listener. At the same time, the challenge for you is to avoid being so implicit or tiptoeing around the mighty life-saving name of Jesus that you never actually use it. Don't "water down" the gospel to the point where it doesn't resemble anything biblical. Both extremes aren't practical, so use your best discretion for the lost audience that you are serving. Write your lyrics with an open Bible and reach the lost for God's kingdom.

A few examples of lost songs are *Don't Waste Your Life* by Lecrae, *Come To The Altar* by Elevation Worship, and *Dear Slim* by KJ52.

3. Church Song

Church songs are the third category of Christian songs which exist to edify, unify and encourage the local and global church. They build up spiritual and moral standards and also develop a deeper understanding of God's character among churchgoers.

One quick way to identify a church song is by listening to its use of inclusive pronouns. When you hear a song properly using pronouns such as **we, us, our** and **ourselves**, which is inclusive language for believers — you are likely listening to or singing a Church Song.

Church Songs can be a collective prayer, a communal lament or encouragement to believers to be bold in faith. These songs help us to uplift one another during difficult times when it's easier to be down. They remind us that the church is united as one family, that Jesus will return for us, and that we have a work to do before He returns called the Great Commission.

As the name suggests, these songs are sung in churches where two or more are gathered and at Christian events around the world attended by billions of believers who make up the body of Christ. So, Church Songs must be written in a way that makes singing along simple for many people at the same time. Chris Tomlin's *Holy Is The Lord*, Delirious' *Shout To The North,* and *Our God Reigns* by Israel Houghton are all examples of Church Songs.

4. Story Song

The fourth category of Christian song is the Story Song. Story Songs work well for sharing your testimony, the testimonies of others and, of course, telling stories.

You can use this category of song to share historical biblical stories, their characters and principles, as well as recent encounters with and miracles by God.

A Story Song for children in Sunday school can be nice and easy, such as the songs *Father Abraham Had Many Sons*, *Zaccheaus, and Noah's Ark* to the more complex story songs for older listeners.

Story Songs are typically written in the past tense, or there's a lyrical theme implying **"once upon a time."** What usually follows is a passing of time (before, during and after) that keeps the narrative moving forward. It's common for story songs to show a contrast between past pain, how God is improving things now, and what a better future will look like because of God's promises.

A famous example of a Story Song is the hymn *Amazing Grace*, written by John Newton. Verse 1 in this song details God's grace that **"saved"** (past tense) a "wretch" like him. The song ends in verse 7 by detailing an image of how we as believers will appear in heaven **"when we've been there ten thousand years"** (future tense).

When you write a Story Song for adults, you may experience the challenge of balancing music with storytelling, which involves characters and plotlines. It can be tricky to put a lot of detail into a catchy melody with easy syllables and a consistent and predictable rhyme scheme.

As a result, Story Songs can become spectator songs, especially during the verses. One person or a few people will usually sing a narrative to a complex melody during the verses as the audience listens and appreciates the story. Spectators usually sing along during the chorus, which is generally written in a way that is simple and more inclusive to balance out any complexity in the verses.

A few examples of story songs are *Prayer Changes by* R Kelly, *Jesus Take The Wheel* by Carrie Underwood and Marvin Sapps' *Never Would Have Made It.*

5. Self Song

The fifth category of Christian song is the Self Song that focuses on affirming your faith in God. Life often gets challenging, and when challenges come, it's easy to get distracted and drift off course away from God. So, it's important to fortify your belief as often as needed, and songs like these are very helpful.

For example, if you are experiencing fear, feeling weak, confused about life and stressed out, your Self Song could echo *2 Timothy 1:7,* "For the Spirit God gave us does not make us timid, but gives us power, love and self-discipline." If you're feeling pain, criticism, condemnation and persecution for sharing your faith, your Self Song could focus on *John 15:21,* which teaches, "They will treat you this way because of my name, for they do not know the one who sent me."

If this is your experience, you're in good company, because it means you are putting your faith into action just as Jesus did. Therefore, you're trying to become more like Christ. So a Self Song to renew your mind could echo *James 1:2,* "Consider it pure joy, my brothers and sisters, whenever you face trials of many kinds because you know that the testing of your faith produces perseverance."

Hearing this kind of biblical truth in a song can uplift you and other believers going through similar trials and tribulations. A Self Song can be one that:

- Laments
- Gives praise and thanksgiving
- Is a prayer that brings petitions to God
- Makes requests known
- Asks for forgiveness and direction

It is HUGELY tempting as a songwriter to write Self Songs which primarily focus on your problems, pain and suffering. It can start to sound whiney and become all about the unholy trinity of **me, myself** and **I** and less about The Holy Trinity of Father, Son and Holy Spirit. There's space and grace to self-express, but avoid whinging and making it all about you. This is not to belittle your problems, but it does magnify how BIG God is in comparison to minuscule issues; this is the right perspective.

For obvious reasons, badly-written Self Songs that are too self-centric, too personal and too specific are often not relatable. Songs with the wrong perspective where **self and problems are bigger than God** will get rejected from being sung at church — and rightfully so.

So write your songs in spirit and in truth, not just to drain negative emotions. Some good examples of Self Songs are *He Turned It* by Tye Tribbett, *Take Me Back* by Dante Bowe and *I Smile* by Kirk Franklin.

Combining Categories

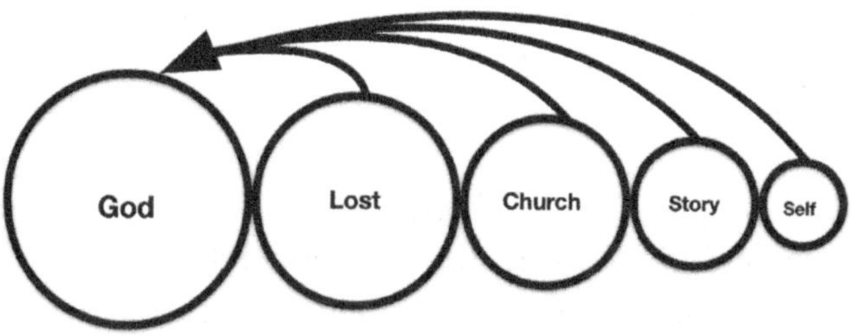

Each category must connect to God

It is quite common for a song to combine two categories at the same time, maybe even three. So it's possible to have a Church Song that's also a Lost Song; a Story Song can be combined with a Self Song, and a God Song can combine to a story and a Self Song.

A God Song is the **ONLY** category of song that can be a standalone category. I'm going to repeat that; A God Song is the only category of song that can work as a standalone song.

Every other category **MUST** connect to God to keep its message and its substance. If you're a little unclear about this, go back to chapter 1 "Odd Without God" to understand some of the reasons why.

Although you'll get opportunities to get creative, I've observed the most successful songs keep it simple with only one or two categories but no more than three. People connect to them better with the least amount of confusion. In other words, write in one, two and maybe three categories every chance you get.

Every Category Has a Home

You may find that songs in Category 1 and 3 **(God** and **Church Songs)** are best suited to Christian believers who attend church regularly. In contrast, songs in Category 2 **(Lost Songs)** are for settings outside the church to reach and relate to those who don't yet believe in God and don't go to church. Songs in Categories 4 and 5 **(Story and Self Song)** can work well both inside and outside church based on their message and intended audience.

Writing a song with a specific message for a specific audience in a specific setting is a sure way to write relevant songs that people will embrace and not reject. In chapter 11, you're going to learn the songwriting steps to focus your lyrics further to make them more relevant, timely and biblical, but don't skip ahead just yet, the coming pages are just as important. Imagine your song being sung generation after generation long after you've gone to be with God. It's possible.

Hopefully, you're starting to see how all these powerful songwriting techniques can stack on top of each other for maximum impact.

Now that you know about the five categories of Christian songs, pronouns will "click in" much easier. Pronouns are the first thing I check when giving constructive feedback to songwriters because misusing pronouns will drive your songs into a ditch.

The following pages will show you how to avoid this mistake, how to use pronouns like a seasoned songwriter, and how pronouns apply to the 5 categories of Christian songs.

THE POWER OF PRONOUNS

If you misuse pronouns, it can drive your song into a ditch because improper use of pronouns has the power to change the meaning of your song in ways you may not intend.

When you pair pronouns properly like you're about to learn, your songs will make sense, and people will be more likely to add them to their repeat playlist.

So what are pronouns? I must confess that when I first started learning to write songs, I felt embarrassed to have forgotten what pronouns are — something simple that I learned in secondary school. Luckily, pronouns are easy to understand and remember.

Here's a recap — a pronoun is a word that helps people understand who the subject or object in your song is. Pronouns are words such as **I, you, he, she, it, they, us** and **we.** When you use one of these words in your lyrics, it signals to listeners who the subject or object is in your song. If you add a second pronoun to your lyrics, it signals a new subject or object and so on. You have to pair your pronouns consistently so that your lyrics explain themselves. If you don't match your pronouns in a consistent way, it will create confusion for listeners.

What follows next are examples of pronouns in three simple songs you may already know:

A. "Read **your** Bible pray every day, and **you'll** grow, grow, grow"
B. "**Our** God is an awesome God **he** reigns with power"
C. "Jesus loves **me**, yes **I** know, for the Bible tells **me** so, little ones to **him** belong, **they** are weak, but **he** is strong."

These three examples show pronouns that are paired consistently. Every time a new pronoun gets added, it introduces a new layer of detail to your song that has to be understood by your listener (who may not know what you're talking about). If you use too many pronoun types in one song without consistency, it creates confusion in the mind of the listener, and remember, a confused mind will always say no to your song by pressing skip to listen to a different song.

Pay attention to the previous three examples:

- Example A uses only one pronoun type — you — in two of its forms **your** and **you'll.** The song *Read Your Bible* is talking to you as the subject of the song, telling you as the listener to read your Bible.
- Example B uses two different pronoun types — we and he — which speaks about **our** God and how **he** reigns.
- Example C uses three pronoun types — I, he and they — which refer to **me** as the singer of the song, Jesus as **Him** and others who belong to Jesus as **they**.

Did you notice how slightly more explanation and slightly more time is needed with every additional pronoun? This is also true for any song you write; your lyrics must be simple enough to explain themselves, and if they're not, you must explain them. Avoid the writing trap of assuming that listeners know what or who you're talking about; often they won't. So make your lyrics frictionless by keeping your pronouns consistent.

How to Pair Pronouns Properly

I created some straightforward guidelines to help you to understand how to pair your pronouns properly and consistently in any song you write. Come back to the table on the next page as many times as you need to until you commit it to memory. It's going to massively help your songwriting.

Pairing Pronouns					
Song Category	Subject Pronoun	Object Pronoun	Posessive Adjective	Possesive Pronoun	Reflexive Pronoun
1. God Song (2nd Person)	You	You	Your	Yours	Yourself
2. Church Song (1st Person Plural)	We	Us	Our	Ours	Ourselves
3. Lost Song (2nd Person)	You	You	Your	Yours	Yourself
4. Self Song (1st Person)	I	Me	My	Mine	Myself
5. Story / God Song (3rd Person Male)	He	Him	His	His	Himself

Pairing pronouns properly

1. Songs with one pronoun type are easiest to understand

The song *Read Your Bible* in Example A is straightforward to understand because it only uses one pronoun type — **You**. Because of that, these kinds of songs are more comfortable to write with consistent pronouns, leaving very little chance of friction for the listener. Another example of a song with one pronoun type is *Agnus Dei* by Michael W. Smith. If you're a new writer, this is the type of song I recommend you write first — a song using only one pronoun type (You) as a praise or worship song to God.

2. Songs with two pronoun types are the most common

You'll probably notice songs with two pronoun types more

than any other because most songs speak of God, how we worship Him and who we are according to Him. You saw two pronoun types earlier in *Our God* shown in Example B, which speaks about **Our** God is an awesome God **He** reigns. Another example of a song with two pronoun types is *Oceans* by Hillsong; notice in this song how the two pronoun types are properly used and stay consistent **I** (me, my, mine), and **You** (your, yours). A different example is the song *You Are Good* by Israel Houghton which uses the two pronoun types **You** (your) and **We**.

3. Songs with three pronoun types need more focus

Pay even closer attention if your song has three pronoun types. Consistency becomes more important because a misplaced pronoun can distract your listeners.

It is **very** easy for you as the writer to assume listeners know what you mean through your lyrics when they don't; this is called writer's assumption. Remember that listeners are not in your head and cannot see the connection your brain is making between your lyrics. Accidental use of pronouns in your songs will happen when your brain makes a connection for you, but your lyrics don't explain that connection for the listener. So stay on top of it because misplaced pronouns are more common when using three pronoun types. Keep them consistent.

On the other hand, when pronouns get paired properly and consistently, it can create super-successful songs such as *Our God* in Example C, *How Great Is Our God* by Chris Tomlin, and *Be Magnified* by Don Moen.

Two examples of inconsistent or misplaced pronoun types can be heard in the song *Way Maker* by Sinach and *What a Beautiful Name* by Hillsong.

Way Maker: Notice how the misplaced pronoun is a little bit jarring as the song establishes two pronoun types (**You** and **Our**) early in verse 1, but jolts by adding a third pronoun type (**I**) slightly out of context.

What a Beautiful Name: Notice how the song establishes two pronoun types **(You** and **Our)** and then adds a third **(Me)** in the chorus and in verse 2. Although it can be said the pronouns were deliberately written like that, I consider them to be misplaced because the meaning of the song doesn't change drastically by changing the pronouns in the chorus and verse 2 from **(My)** to **(Our)**. Changing them from **(My)** to **(Our)** would make the pronouns more intact, more consistent than currently written and still remain singable in the same way. That's why I think of them as misplaced pronouns. Are you getting it?

This is not a criticism of the two songs, just an objective observation to raise your awareness. Fortunately, both songs are massively successful and loved by hundreds of millions all around the world, so there's grace if you make mistakes (and you will, so embrace it); just do your best to minimise inconsistent and improper use of pronouns.

4. Avoid writing songs with four or more pronoun types

That's all there is to be said about this. I couldn't think of or find a song example with four pronoun types, but if you do insist on writing one, you will have to work extra hard and write very skillfully not to leave any lyrical loose ends that could confuse people. My suggestion is to avoid four pronoun types.

5. Your first and second pronoun types should guide you

Pay attention to the first two pronoun types that appear in your song. They're like the first two domino pieces that will impact all the rest of your lyrics. Before you introduce a third pronoun type, stop and ask yourself: "Why is it necessary?" For example, *Way Maker* by Sinach, which jumped from **our** (inclusive) to **I** (exclusive), could have used the first two pronouns in the song as a guide for the pronouns that follow. It could have sounded something like this "**1. you** are here moving in **2.our** midst (inclusive), **3.we** (inclusive) worship **you**...". Looking at the first and second pronoun types could have made this obvious to the writers.

Today there are other versions of *Way Maker* online covered by different artists who saw the error and made the edit from **I** to **we.** Remember — great songs are not written, they're rewritten.

More Pronouns

There are other pronouns you need to know about. Although they may feature less in your music, it's good to be aware of them and when to use them. I chose to group these 3rd person pronoun types separately to make them a little bit easier to understand in their context.

Pairing Pronouns					
Song Category	**Subject Pronoun**	**Object Pronoun**	**Posessive Adjective**	**Possesive Pronoun**	**Reflexive Pronoun**
Story Song (3rd Person Female)	She	Her	Her	Hers	Herself
3rd Person & Thing (Plural)	They	Them	Their	Theirs	Themselves
3rd Thing	It	It	Its	Not used	Itself

How to pair 3rd person pronouns

The first pronoun type in the table above, **She**, gets used in songs that tell a story, such as Carrie Underwood's *Jesus Take The Wheel.* The pronoun type, **They,** can feature in a mix of different song categories; one example is Hillsong's *Tell The World.* Lastly, the pronoun type, **It**, can also feature in a mix of songs, such as in Kirk Franklin's song *Something About The Name Jesus,* where the object of the song is the name Jesus; the lyrics later go on to say "**It** is the sweetest name I know."

Remember, songs can be thought of as a dialogue between two people or a story told simply. So group your pronouns to convey a conversation or tell a story effectively with little to no friction for the listener.

Now you know what pronouns are and how to match them properly and consistently so that you don't drive your song into a ditch. You also know that your song is like a dialogue between two people or telling a story in a simple way. Next, you'll learn about timing, or when your song will connect best with certain listeners.

THE 5 STAGES OF FAITH

In the previous pages, you learned the power of speaking specifically to specific listeners. In these next few pages, you're going to learn about the power of timing.

A songwriting approach that can help you is to focus on helping people at different stages of their faith through your songs. When you think about the stages of faith, it's similar to real-life; a newborn baby has very different needs than a teenager, who has different needs than a mature adult. It's the same in spiritual growth and maturity. A new born-again Christian saved just last Tuesday has very different needs than a Christian who's been saved for 12 years, which is different to the needs of a mature Christian who helps others to mature as Christians.

For clarification, here are brief definitions of The 5 Stages of Faith as outlined by John Putman's ministry. These definitions are not for you to label people or use these labels as absolute truth. They are simply a tool to help you reflect on your own experiences and better relate to the experiences of others so you can write God-centred songs that serves their needs based on where they are.

The 5 stages of faith

The 5 Stages of Faith

The 5 Stages of Faith include:

1. Non-believer: People at this stage of faith have not yet accepted Jesus as their Lord and Saviour because they may have **never** heard of Jesus Christ or God. Some may reject God, others may be seeking God, and others may consider themselves to be a "spiritual" person, but struggle to define what that means.

Some may even claim to know God and consider themselves a "Christian" based on their country of birth or their country's main religion when, in reality, they are their own god.

2. Beginner: Beginners have accepted Jesus Christ, but haven't moved much past that point. They can be new believers, or they may be stuck-in-the-mud Christians who haven't progressed for a long time or at all. Life at this point is generally all about them and their needs.

3. Believer: Believers are growing their relationship with God and are also beginning to grow in their relationship with other Christians. They are applying God's word in their life and allowing others to walk beside them in their journey with Jesus. However, life is still mostly about them and their needs, comfort and their preferences.

4. Follower: People at this stage of faith are making a **significant** shift from being self-centred to more others-centred. They're beginning to understand their role as a giver rather than a taker, ministering to others, putting others first and being not only readers of the Bible, but doers of God's word. They're moving from selfish to selfless in the true sense of the word. They don't think less of themselves; they think of themselves less.

5. Disciple: People at this stage have a solid understanding of God's word and a deep, abiding relationship of love with the Father. They are living out God's word by faith in their life daily. They are others-centred, and they choose to fully depend on God even though they're capable people. They're able to bring others to salvation as mature disciples of Jesus, either actively through their ministry or passively through their life's example.

Change, Not Age

Please notice that the 5 Stages of Faith have **nothing** to do with how old someone is; instead, they're based on spiritual maturity. And remember, maturity is based on the willingness to change and not on the age of a person. That's how it's possible to be juvenile at 60 years old and also possible to be mature at 16. Spiritual maturity will vary from person to person; people are complex and can be at various stages of faith at different times in their lives.

So, as you write songs with an open Bible in the spirit of worshipping God, with a heart of ministering to people as inspired by the Holy Spirit, remember that each of these stages of faith has different needs. Writing your song in this way based on timing and seasons of faith can help you create songs that almost everyone can relate to and will always be needed and appreciated by listeners.

It's like Christmas songs; from mid-October to late December almost every speaker and headphone closest to you is playing Christmas songs. Why? Because the timing is right and it's the season. People are more receptive to them, are seeking them out and appreciate them more.

Now imagine having an equivalent for people's faith — for those who don't know God, those who have hit a crisis, those who just got saved, those who are stuck in their faith and don't know what to do next, those who are activating their faith and are starting to "get it," those who are selfless and want others on their journey of faith, and those who may need to be reminded not to grow weary of doing the good work of maturing other Christians. The possibilities are endless.

Who's on Your Heart?

Because of who God has put on your heart, your own experiences and the experiences of people you know, you may resonate more with one or multiple stages of faith. I strongly suggest you start by writing a song for a stage of faith where you had your biggest breakthrough.

Ask yourself: "What spiritual challenges is this person facing at this stage? What are they happy or excited about? What pain and frustration are they feeling with their faith? What encouragement do they need to lift their spirit? What spiritual and life milestone is coming up or being celebrated? What biblical verse can I write about to help them conquer their fears?"

I am a fan of this writing method because it acknowledges the milestone or problems of the person and presents God the Father, Son and Holy Spirit as the solution. A lot of what you'll do as a songwriter is to have empathy for and relate to people — to put yourself in their shoes or remind yourself what it was like when you used to be in that same place — and write songs for where people are. They will connect with it, and when they do, just offer God as the solution. Boom! That's powerful stuff!

What's also great is that some people only listen to Hip-Hop, some only listen to Gospel music, and some listen to Country and Folk music, while others listen to Rock and Contemporary Christian Music. What this means for you is that you will get plenty of opportunities to reach people in the genre that you write with a life-saving message. Even if the same or similar message exists in a different genre, only you can reach the people on your heart because they don't listen to those different genres and won't connect with other artists. But they do listen to your genre and will connect better with you. So don't delay, start writing today or as soon as possible.

People also speak different languages, so there's plenty of room for all of us globally as believers, worship leaders, Christian musicians and lyricists to reach people at certain stages, in certain genres and certain languages with the Bible's message of hope and salvation.

YOUR KEY MINDSET

At the heart of it, the 5 categories of Christian songs and the 5 stages of faith represents a particular group of people who are going through a particular season or are on their way (often unknowingly) towards a series of milestones.

Write Songs That Serve

When you're feeling stuck about what to write and you have zero song ideas, my hunch is that in those moments you are thinking about yourself and your need for creative self-expression. I encourage you to think of your music as a ministry that meets the needs of those you are called to serve.

That's the key mindset — think of your music firstly, as a way to worship God; secondly, as a way to minister to other people; and thirdly, as a means of creative self-expression, and in that sequence. People who put that sequence in reverse order — 3, 2, 1 — eventually experience creative constipation or a music drought because honestly, how much self-expression can you really put out before you run dry? My guess is not very much, because it's less about getting and more about giving your worship, 'It is more blessed to give than to receive.' *(Act 20:35).*

So, if your mindset before writing each song is: "How many people can I serve through my music? What do they need to hear to be led to God? What problems can I help to solve or alleviate through my lyrics?" you will get endless answers because there are almost eight billion people on earth and each has a laundry list of problems. This means you can have a laundry list of song ideas.

Making this songwriting shift is significant, and when you truly get it and change to the mindset of **music as a ministry,** you'll get overwhelmed and won't be able to keep up with good ideas of what to write next.

Burning Passion or Heavy Burdens

A way to help you identify who God has put on your heart to serve (if you don't already know) is to remind or ask yourself what excites you the most and what offends you the most? If for example, God put young people on your heart who don't know Jesus, writing Lost Songs (for non-believers) would be where you could start.

If perhaps you have a heart to encourage your local church, you may want to write a Church Song. Maybe you've struggled and suffered in life, which has led you to have a firm faith in God that isn't easily shaken; if so, a Self Song (for followers and disciples) may be what you need to write to affirm their faith and encourage them on their towards to a milestone. And if your heart is often thinking on the goodness, wonders and miracles of God, you may want to start by writing a God Song.

I've noticed that many Christians either live life with a burning passion or a heavy burden on their hearts and sometimes both. That passion or burden usually points towards a particular group of people who they are called to serve. Can you relate? What burning passion and heavy burden has God put on your heart?

When you think about God, the lost, the church, testimonies you've heard, as well as your personal faith, what gets your spirit going? Start your songwriting based on that answer.

KEY POINTS FROM HOW TO WRITE LYRICS PART 2

Long Words Loses You Listeners

Most people need a dictionary to understand 6, 7 and 8-syllable words. Avoid long words in your lyrics. The upper limit of what's really practical for your song lyrics is five syllables.

Syllables

Single-syllable words are your friends; make them your go-to writing tool. Use as many as you can in a song because it helps your song to be more singable. Remember also to count syllables per line if writing Hymns.

Pair Your Pronouns Properly

Misused and misplaced pronouns will make other people edit your song mistakes for you. Commit the two pronoun type tables to memory; it will help you to write more consistently with little to no errors.

There Are 5 Categories of Christian Songs

Know the 5 categories by heart and know what category of song you are writing or combining. Each category of Christian song is like a ministry in itself. If you write songs in one category more often than not, God has likely put that group of people or ministry on your heart. Explore it further and deeper.

There's a Song for Every Stage of Faith

Empathy will play a big part in your songwriting. Think of where someone is in their spiritual journey and write a song that helps them to connect to God from that place, there's power in timing. Your song will be more potent and authentic to that listener if you've been where they are, and they can relate to your lyrics. You can also use the experiences of others to relate and write a song.

Your Music Is a Ministry That Worships God and Serves People

When you have writer's block and no ideas are coming to you, just shift the focus off yourself and onto people you can serve through music. God has either put a burning passion or heavy burden on your heart towards a particular group of people. Who are they?

CHAPTER 5
THE 7 SONG STRUCTURES

Previously you learned about the major and minor building blocks needed to arrange your song. In this part of the book, you will learn in what order to sequence those building blocks for maximum impact. These sequences, also known as "Structures,", "Forms" or "Arrangements" are proven to work for all genres. They will help the listeners and singers of your songs to connect with your song's message while smoothly transitioning from one part of your song to the other.

It's worth noting that these structures have been used over decades or have evolved over hundreds of years and they still work today. As a result, they go by one or multiple names in different countries, which can create some confusion about what to call them.

Luckily, this book is your practical songwriting guide that avoids unnecessary music theory that would slow down your progress. Instead, this book aims to use the simplest, practical and relevant names to help you get songwriting results as soon as possible. Rest assured, regardless of their different names around the world; these structures are the same.

The names of the seven song structures are:

1. Verse/Chorus

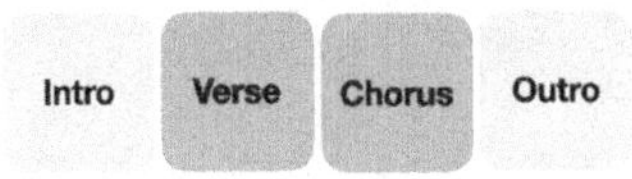

"Verse/Chorus" is a simple structure that most people can sing, understand and remember. It goes by that name because it only has two major building blocks — the verse and the chorus, and each block has its unique melody. At first, it may seem as though it's limiting to have so few parts in a song, but writing a simple two-section song forces you to focus on the key message of your song and not distract from it or dilute it with too many other messages. You can use this structure to write songs for many settings, such as Sunday School, group worship and more. The Verse/Chorus structure is used in many songs, such as *Oh Happy Day* by the Edwin Hawkins Singers, *Agnus Dei* by Michael W Smith, *He Is Exalted* by Twila Paris, and *Shout To The Lord* by Hillsong. *Shout to the Lord* seems like a long song, but is simply an extended version of the Verse/Chorus structure made up of two verses in a row followed by two choruses in a row (V/V/C/C). This simple structure works well whether you're a beginner or advanced songwriter.

2. Theme and Variation

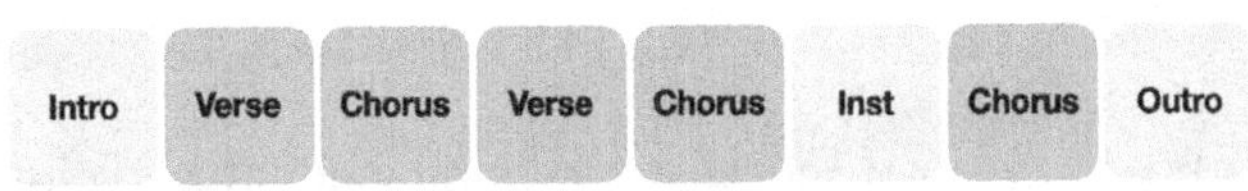

The "Theme & Variation" structure builds on the Verse/Chorus structure. It goes by that name because of how it allows you to alternate between the verse and the chorus in a predictable pattern.

In the verse, you can establish a structural, lyrical and musical **theme** followed by **the variety** of the chorus. Because there are two or more verses in this structure, you get the opportunity to use them for diving deeper into detail with the writing techniques you learned earlier for major building blocks. The interlude in this structure is often used for a solo or a breakdown. Examples of this structure can be heard in *Smile Again* by Kirk Franklin, and *I'm Alive* by K-Anthony.

3. ABC

The "ABC" structure builds on the Theme and Variation structure by inserting a "Bridge" section. It goes by the name ABC because it's based on a concept that labels the verses as part "A," the choruses as part "B" and the bridge as part "C." The interlude or instrumental can go either before or after the bridge; it's your choice. After the bridge, you may also choose to add a verse or chorus; both variations work. You can hear examples of this structure in the songs *Reckless Love* by Cory Asbury, as well as *Oceans* and *What a Beautiful Name* By Hillsong.

4. Compound

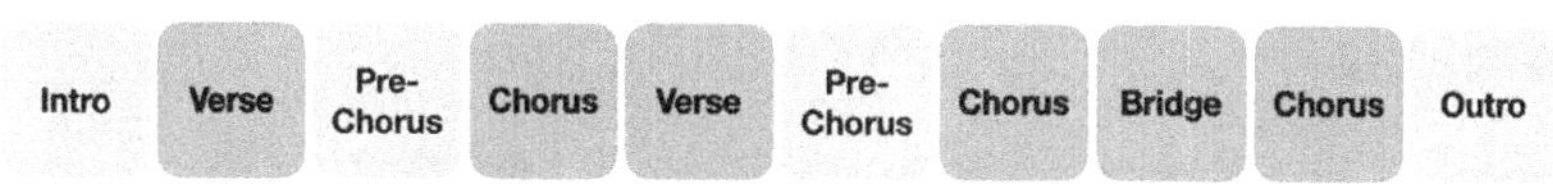

The "Compound" structure can also be called a hybrid structure because although it may be commonplace to hear it in today's modern music, it came into existence over many decades through songwriters who combined simple song forms to create a compound. This structure inserts a minor block called a Pre-chorus just before the chorus. You can use the Pre-chorus to create a musical and lyrical lift or to build tension. You may choose to include a double bridge in this structure, and it would still be an effective structure for your song. Examples of this structure are songs such as *Majesty* by Delirious, *Lord You Are Good* by Israel Houghton, and *Ever Be* by Bethel Music.

5. American Popular Song

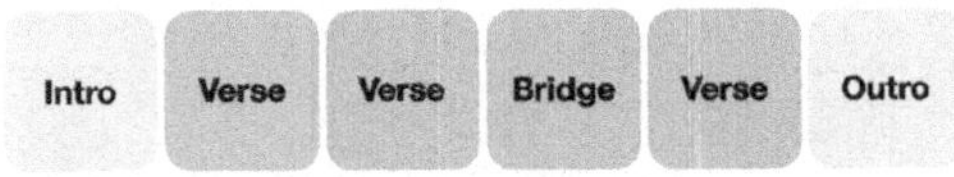

The "American Popular Song" structure is most characterised by not having a chorus. It was most used from roughly 1910 to the 1960s when it started to fade out of popularity. But it is still being used today. It goes by that name because it was the structure used in a lot of mainstream music made in the U.S.A during the early to mid-20th century. This structure features in songs such as *Great Balls Of Fire* by Jerry Lee Lewis, *All I Have To Do Is Dream* by the Everly Brothers and in Broadway musical shows such as *The Wizard of Oz* and *Guys & Dolls*. This structure was also used in Motown pop-gospel songs such as the Stevie Wonder version of *Swing Low Sweet Chariot*, *Oh Happy Day* by the Edwin Hawkins Singers and *Wholly Holy* by Marvin Gaye. The American Popular Song structure is still being used today in the Jazz and Blues music genres.

6. Rondo

The "Rondo" structure is best characterised by starting with and ending the song with the chorus. As a structure, it gets straight to the point with a no-nonsense approach compared to other structures because the hook (**the thing that listeners**

love) is right at the start. The image above shows what a 7-part Rondo structure looks like. You can shorten it into a 6-part version (C/V/C/I/B/C) or make it an even shorter 5-part version (C/V/C/B/C). I've also heard extended versions of the Rondo structure work well with multiple solos at live shows. It's a versatile structure that can be very engaging both for the singers and the listeners of your songs as long as you do your job of writing great lyrics. Examples of this structure can be heard in *Shackles* by Mary Mary, *I'll Find You* by Lecrae Ft. Tori Kelly, and *10,000 Reasons* by Matt Redman.

7. One-Part Song

The One-part Song — also called the "Strophic" structure — is unique because it only has one major building block: the verse. Historically speaking, this is one of the earliest song structures dating back to when popular poems were first being set to music. It was the structure used in almost all hymns until the 19th century, when refrains and choruses started to grow in popularity. This structure has the nicknames the "Storytelling" and the "Balladeer" structure because it gives maximum room for detail and telling stories compared to other structures. Although this structure isn't as popular as it used to be, it does still get used and can be heard in Hymns, Hip Hop, Folk and Country music.

Since this structure doesn't have a chorus, in hymns the song title tends to come from the first line of verse 1 like in the hymns *When I Survey The Wondrous Cross* and *In Christ Alone.* Usually, the same melody is repeated for each of the verses with different lyrics. The only time lyrics may repeat is when a refrain is used in the verses, such as in the hymn *Take It To The Lord In*

Prayer, where a lyrical or musical refrain is found at the end of each verse. Refrains can also be placed at the start or middle of your verse; it's up to you. In Hip Hop, this one-part-song structure is used by artists such as Lecrae, Andy Mineo and Trip Lee, who freestyle rap in 8, 16, 24 or 32 bar verses to deliver their message, make a point or tell a story. Folk And Country music artists use this structure in a similar way with or without refrains.

The challenge with this structure is that boredom can set in quickly with your listeners because of a repetitive melody or rhyme scheme. As a result, you need to write very compelling lyrics and engaging music to captivate and keep the attention of your listeners. You can hear the one-part-song structure in the Motown song *People Get Ready* by Curtis Mayfield, as well as the hymn *Amazing Grace* by John Newton.

Other Structures

Are there other song structures besides these seven? Of course! However, these seven are the most proven, robust and popular structures that will help you to get the most immediate songwriting results. It's natural to want to improvise, explore and discover what creative results you can come up with that aren't listed here. Still, as a general rule of thumb, I recommend that you first master these seven before venturing off to experiment.

KEY POINTS FROM THE 7 SONG STRUCTURES

Use the 7 Song Structures

It's okay if your song doesn't take shape when you first start writing. But do your best to put your song into 1 of the 7 structures that fits the best. These structures go by different names in different countries but are the same. Their names are:

1. **Verse/Chorus:** V/C
2. **Theme and Variation:** V/C/V/C/I/C
3. **ABC:** V/C/V/C/I/B/C
4. **Compound:** V-PC/C/V-PC/C/B/C
5. **American Popular Song:** V/V/B/V
6. **Rondo:** C/V/C/V/C/B/C
7. **One-part Song:** V/V/V

Model What Works

These 7 song structures are proven to work over decades and over multiple genres. Write using one song structure and get familiar with it first (I recommend starting with Theme and Variation) before mastering the next song structure.

Once you've written several songs using one song structures, explore the other structures.

CHAPTER 6
HOW TO WRITE A HIT SONG

Your Motive Matters

I have a confession to make to you. I want to write hit songs. I want to write songs that win awards, and if you're reading this chapter, my guess is that you want that, too. So that's not really my confession. The real confession is that for a time when I was younger, that's all I wanted. There's a part of me that wanted fame, fortune, accolades, recognition and validation, but the problem is, that had almost nothing to do with God and almost everything to do with me — my ego, my pride, my wants, my selfishness. In short, I was prepared to use something intended for worshipping God — music — for self-glorification, fame and personal gain.

Does that sound to you like anyone in the Bible? Scary! It's a bitter pill to swallow, but it's the truth. But God is good. He did not allow me to have those things when I was younger; I wouldn't have had the maturity to handle it. In many ways, it's the best thing that never happened to me.

Now that I'm a little older, I can reflect with a

perspective from the Holy Spirit to see things from a new vantage point. It is not a bad thing to want accolades, recognition or validation. The problem came when I made those things my primary and only focus. I could dress it up in different ways, but the truth is my motives were corrupt when they were driven by self-gain. None of us can hide or disguise our motives because God says in the Bible, "The Lord does not look at the things people look at. People look at the outward appearance, but the Lord looks at the heart." *(1 Sam 16:7)*. God also says that "I the Lord search the heart and examine the mind, to reward each person according to their conduct, according to what their deeds deserve." *(Jer 17:10)*.

It's You Vs. You

When writing lyrics, pursue your personal best. The Bible says whatever you do, work at it with all your heart, as working for the Lord, and not for human masters, since you know you will receive an inheritance from the Lord as a reward. It is the Lord Christ you are serving. *(Col 3:23)*. The keyword here is **personal** best, which means don't compare yourself to others. You should **only** compare yourself to yourself and surpass your personal best from yesterday for the glory of God. That's it. As you set out to glorify God, God will search your heart and examine your mind. He'll see your conduct and your deeds, and He'll reward you deservedly with accolades, validation and recognition — the by-products of excellence. Otherwise, God will wreck your plans before your plans wreck you. See the difference? It's the same outcome, but a different motive. So ask yourself, **why** do you want to write award-winning hit songs?

When you understand and live out that critical distinction, you can get on with writing a hit song. I never used to believe this, but writing songs that win awards and become hits is simple — not easy, but simple. When you master the writing techniques in this book and submit your songs every year during the intake period, eventually you will win. But your songs must be good and you must keep improving.

How to Write a Hit Song

One of the quickest ways to write award-winning hit songs is to be coached by someone who's already won those awards or chart position you seek. If these types of people are not within your reach, the next best thing is to **model** hit songs and award-winning songs that are already successful. **Do not copy.** I can't emphasise this enough: **don't copy others.** However, you can **model** parameters of hit songs and these three quick steps will help:

Step 1

Pick three songs in the same genre that resonate with the people you're trying to serve through music ministry.

Step 2

Make sure the three songs have either won awards or were in the top 10 chart position in that genre.

> **Tip:** hit songs have roughly three million views or more on YouTube.

Step 3

Identify the music parameters that are common in all three songs and emulate those parameters either as an average between the three songs or choose only one song to model.

The music parameters you can model include:

Key

If an award-winning song is in the key of C, your song can be in the same key. It's allowed.

Tempo

If a successful song is 115 beats per minute, your song can also be 115 bpm.

Time signature

If a song that resonates with people is in the time signature of 4/4 or 6/8, your song can model that time signature without issues.

Chord progression

You can emulate the chord progression of a hit song, for example, C/G/Am/F. You can also use the same progression in a different key for singing comfort, for example: chord I/V/vi/IV also known as the 1st/5th/Minor 6th/4th. What chords communicate was covered in chapter 3 and there are chord progressions in the back of this book to help you. Review them to kick start your writing.

Category

You can write a God song, Lost song, Church song, Story song or a Self song. You can also combine two categories, like the hit song you want to emulate. The 5 categories of Christian songs were covered in chapter 4.

Topic

If there's a specific topic that resonates with your listeners during their stage of faith, you can write about that topic or another relevant one that your listeners connect with. Read more about stages of faith in chapter 4 and topics to write about in chapter 11, but don't skip ahead just yet.

Genre

Listeners who you are trying to serve through songs will resonate with a certain genre more than another. Know what that genre is. If it's not a genre you write, collaborate with someone who does.

Collaboration is covered at length in chapter 2. Remember: a good message will resonate in multiple genres.

Song length

If a hit song on a playlist, radio or people's phones is 3 minutes and 30 seconds long, your song should also be more or less the same length.

Song structure

If a song is going viral (see chapter 8), pay attention not only to the structure (see chapter 5), but also to the number of bars/ measures in each major and minor building block as covered in chapters 3 and 4 and emulate them.

These 9 parameters are plenty enough to point you in the right direction of writing potential hit songs.

Collect Hit Song Recipes

Again I must stress, don't duplicate, but do emulate what works. Those parameters of music can be used in a similar way without copying or breaking any copyright laws. After a while, you'll notice that "hit songs" and "award-winning songs" have a format, a formula and a recipe that's consistent and that works. It's like going to a restaurant and having a great meal that you love so much, you end up asking the chef for the recipe. The chef is kind enough to write down the ingredient list, the ratios to use, how to cook each ingredient, how long to cook it for and how many it will feed. When you go home, you'll be able to replicate the same meal and get better results each time you cook that meal. Do you get it? Your songwriting is the same. Pay attention to and start collecting hit song recipes that work and then try them out at home.

Don't Be a Copycat

Its common sense that the more parameters you emulate in a song, the more your song will sound like the original. To avoid being a copycat, you can mix up one or more parameters in the following ways:

- **Tempo:** Speeding up or slowing down the pace of the song
- **Key:** Using a different key or adding a key change
- **Instrument:** If the original features a guitar, use a keyboard
- **Chord progression:** Use the same chords, but change the sequence

These are just four examples, but changing these and other parameters will make enough of a noticeable difference to keep your song in the sweet spot for your listeners.

Avoid This

Do not emulate, duplicate or copy the following under any circumstances:

Melody: Your notes must not be the same sequence as the song you are referencing. This is a sure way to invite negative comparison, confusion and spicy problems from the writers of the original song. The bigger and more successful your song becomes, the bigger and spicier your problems will also be, so **do not** copy anyone's melody.

Lyrics: This should be a no-brainer. **Do not** copy someone else's lyrics and add them into your original song. The only time you're allowed to copy lyrics is when they come from the Bible or 70 years after the death of a writer, which is when copyright expires.

Singing style: This parameter is about **how** you sound when you sing. You won't get into much trouble with this as you would with the previous two, but avoid sounding like someone else. Just be yourself. It's easy to be influenced by those we admire, especially when starting out, but eventually, you should develop your own "voice." See chapter 3 for more information about how to develop your voice.

Start Small and Win Big

If you follow the steps above to write a song, you will have written a song that could be a hit and could win awards; the only way to find out is to submit your song. At this point, you may be thinking of the biggest, most well-known awards such as the Grammys. However, remember there are other awards along the way.

You can submit your song to awards that are local, regional, national or international — and you can win these more easily than the big ones. Some awards are free to enter and submit, some may require payment, some may give you a certificate or a trophy, and others give cash and prizes. You may need to be a member to submit to some awards, whereas others are open to the public. You can submit the same song and album under multiple categories such as best album, best song, best new writer or artist and best in your genre. Each awarding body has its own conditions and deadlines, so find out the details and then submit.

Entering the Charts

The same song or album you used to submit for awards can also be used to enter the charts. Just like when submitting for awards, you can achieve a chart position on smaller and unofficial charts like Christian music blogs and playlists on YouTube; these will be easier wins for you. They have also become great ways for music fans to discover new music, and they can act as minor stream sources that flow into the official charts as more people discover and love your songs. Submit your songs to as many unofficial blogs and playlists; there are equivalent charts in a lot of languages, so you can find the ones that originate from your country or are in your language. Simply do a search on Google for Christian music blogs and playlists by genre or language; the owners of these blogs are usually looking for good music and will be glad to hear from you.

You can then build up to entering playlists like Apple and Spotify Christian music and then work up to the well-known charts like the billboard charts or the national Christian chart in your country. Each chart, blog and playlist has conditions and deadlines, so do a little research, find out the details and then submit your songs.

Submitting to and winning smaller awards and chart position each year will give you the experience, confirmation and confidence to submit and win bigger and more competitive awards such as the GMA Dove Awards, The Stellar Awards, Brit Awards, The Grammys or the national equivalent in your country. In brief, write great songs, submit, win, go bigger the following year and repeat.

Keep Learning Every Year

To help you better understand what successful songs sound like in your genre, I have included a selection of hit songs that climbed the charts as well as songs that have won accolades and awards over the years. You can find these on the next page. If you've never heard them before, I recommend that you listen to them. I also recommend that you keep an ear open for the annual winners in your genre or category and pay attention to new trends and those trends that never change.

Celebrate Your Progress

I have met writers and musicians who have zero desire to write hit songs, win awards, receive airplay or go viral and that's okay. If that's you, I suggest having at least seven other ways to define your progress. Imagine writing a song that does really well. What does that success look like to you? List seven things you can track or measure, so you know when you're progressing and celebrate your wins along the way.

Well done! You've finished reading chapter 6 and you're past the halfway point in this book. Be proud of yourself knowing that many who started at Chapter 1 have not got this far. This makes you an action taker, which means you'll get the songwriting results you want by putting this information into action. You've come this far, keep reading until the end to uncover even more secret songwriting techniques.

AWARD-WINNING SONGS AND CHART TOPPERS

What follows for the next few pages is a list of songs that have won one or multiple awards and reached high positions in their respective charts. These accolades are not specific to any period of time; they were awarded over several years. The songs will be grouped by genre and show music parameters that you can emulate in your songwriting. You may want to start paying attention to these and other parameters for award-winning songs both now and in the future.

The parameters are, awards won, chart position, category of christian song, song duration, key message, tempo, time signature, key and song structure.

Urban Gospel Music

Award Won	Artist	Song	Chart Position	Category	Length	Key Message	Tempo	Time Signature	Key	Song Structure
Grammy	Kirk Franklin	Love Theory	#1	God / Self Song	4:11	Jesus is the only hero I need	97 bpm	4/4	D♭ Major	Theme & Variation
Billboard Music Awards	Koryn Hawthorne	Won't He Do It	#1	God / Self Song	3:33	God will keep his word to you	140 bpm	4/4	A Minor	ABC
Billboard Music Awards	Kirk Franklin	Wanna Be Happy?	#1	Lost / Self Song	4:32	Wanna be happy? Give it all to God	84 bpm	4/4	C Major	Compound
Grammy	Mary Mary	Go Get It	#4	Self Song	3:08	It's your time, go get it	93 bpm	4/4	D♭ Major	ABC
Grammy	Tori Kelly	Never Alone	#4	Self Song	4:44	Even through pain, God calls me his own	91 bpm	4/4	D♭ Major	Compound

Christian Pop Music

Award Won	Artist	Song	Chart Position	Category	Length	Key Message	Tempo	Time Signature	Key	Song Structure
Dove / GMA	Lauren Daigle	Trust In You	#1	God / Self Song	3:34	I trust you even when I don't sense you	88 bpm	4/4	A Major	ABC
Dove / GMA	Tauren Wells	Hills and Valleys	#3	Self / God Song	4:12	In my success & failures I will worship God	79 bpm	4/4	D Major	ABC
Dove / GMA	For King And Country	Run Wild	#37	Self Song	4:01	You're created wild & free	130 bpm	4/4	G Minor	ABC
Dove / GMA	Laura Story	Blessings	#1	Church / God Song	4:55	What if your trials are your blessings	116 bpm	4/4	B major	Compound
Dove / GMA	Toby Mac	City On Our Knees	#1	Lost / God Song	4:42	Let sinners & saints bow & worship	156 bpm	4/4	C Major	ABC

Contemporary Christian Music

Award Won	Artist	Song	Chart Position	Category	Length	Key Message	Tempo	Time Signature	Key	Song Structure
Grammy	Matt Redman	10,000 Reasons	#2	God / Self Song	4:21	Bless the lord	145 bpm	4/4	G Major	Rondo
Grammy	Hillsong	What a Beautiful Name	#1	God / Self Song	5:42	The name of Jesus is beautiful	136 bpm	4/4	D Major	ABC
Dove / GMA	Bethel Music	No Longer Slaves	#19	God / Self Song	6:09	I'm not a slave to fear, I'm God's Child	148 bpm	4/4	B♭ Major	ABC
Grammy	Chris Tomlin	Our God	#1	God / Church Song	4:46	If god is for us who can be against us?	105 bpm	4/4	B Major	ABC
BMI Christian Music Awards	Phil Wickham	This is Amazing Grace	#2	God / Self Song	4:38	There's a love that God only knows	144 bpm	4/4	B♭ Major	ABC

Country Gospel Music

Award Won	Artist	Song	Chart Position	Category	Length	Key Message	Tempo	Time Signature	Key	Song Structure
Dove / GMA	Josh Turner	I saw The Light	#2	Lost / Story Song	3:22	A sinner who saw the light	92 bpm	4/4	E♭ Major	Theme & Variation
Grammy	Jason Crabb	Expect The Unexpected	#6	Story / God Song	3:44	God does many miracles	180 bpm	4/4	C Major	Theme & Variation
Grammy	Reba McEntire	Back To God	#1	Lost / God Song	4:37	Lets give our world back to God	148 bpm	4/4	F# Major	Compound
Dove / GMA	Zach Williams	Old Church Choir	#1	Self Song	3:18	Nothing's gonna steal my joy	104 bpm	4/4	C Major	Theme & Variation
Dove / Grammy	Diamond Rio	The Reason	#17	Self / God Song	3:09	Nothing without You	140 bpm	4/4	C Major	Theme & Variation

Christian Hip Hop Music

Award Won	Artist	Song	Chart Position	Category	Length	Key Message	Tempo	Time Signature	Key	Song Structure
Grammy	Lecrae	Messengers	#7	Church Song	3:53	We are called, spread the message	90 bpm	4/4	G Major	Rondo
Dove / GMA	KB	100	#18	Self Song	3:42	I'm committed to God 100%	130 bpm	4/4	G Major	Theme & Variation
Dove / GMA	Social Club Misfits	War Cry	#32	Church / Self Song	3:11	Church it's our time to rise up	112 bpm	4/4	G Major	Rondo
Dove / GMA	NF	Oh Lord	#20	Self Song	3:18	God, do you see us?	88 bpm	4/4	F Major	Theme & Variation
Dove / GMA	Lecrae	Tell The World	#20	Self Song	3:37	I'll tell the world about God	130 bpm	4/4	F# Major	Rondo

Traditional Gospel Music

Award Won	Artist	Song	Chart Position	Category	Length	Key Message	Tempo	Time Signature	Key	Song Structure
Dove / GMA	Marvin Sapp	Close	#1	Self Song	4:26	I'm close to my blessings	120 bpm	6/8	A♭ Major	Rondo
Dove / GMA	Tamela Mann	Change Me	#2	Self Song	6:06	Make me more like you	90 bpm	4/4	F# Major	Verse / Chorus
Grammy	Tasha Cobbs	This Is A Move	#4	Church / God Song	7:25	You are a miraculous God	94 bpm	6/8	A♭ Major	ABC
Dove / GMA	Israel Houghton	How Awesome is Our God	#5	God / Church Song	7:21	Our God is awesome	82 bpm	4/4	G Minor	Rondo
Dove / GMA	Erica Campbell	A Little More Jesus	#3	Self Song	4:00	I need more of Jesus	97 bpm	4/4	F Minor	Rondo

Christian Rock Music

Award Won	Artist	Song	Chart Position	Category	Length	Key Message	Tempo	Time Signature	Key	Song Structure
Dove / GMA	Audio Adrenaline	Lift	#12	God / Self Song	3:54	You bless me & I lift you up	126 bpm	4/4	D♭ Major	Theme & Variation
Dove / GMA	Francesca Battistelli	Beautiful	#3	Self Song	3:25	It's beautiful how you save me from sin	132 bpm	4/4	E Minor	ABC
Dove / GMA	David Crowder Band	Everything Glorious	#2	God / Self Song	3:47	You make all things glorious	94 bpm	4/4	D♭ Major	ABC
Grammy	Third Day	Revelation	#6	Self Song	5:31	Give me revelation	158 bpm	4/4	D Major	ABC
Grammy	Jonny Lang	Turn Around	#35	Story Song	4:41	Turn away from bad choices	113 bpm	4/4	B Minor	ABC

KEY POINTS FROM HOW TO WRITE A HIT SONG

Your Motive Matters

Why do you want to write a hit song? Is it for fame, money or recognition? If that's what drives you, you're headed for predictable disappointment. Make it about God first; let those things be a byproduct.

Outdo Yourself

Whatever you do, work at it with all your heart, as working for the Lord. Never compare yourself to **anyone**. Every day should be you today versus you yesterday.

The Clues Are All Around You

Every time someone writes a hit song with age-old proven techniques that you've learned in this book, or wins an award using new techniques, they leave a recipe about how they did it. All you have to do is emulate their success. But **never copy**.

Collect Recipes

Make a note of songs that catch your ear — songs that connect with the listeners you're trying to serve through your music ministry and refer back to them when writing.

Copyright Laws Exist for a Reason

Avoid emulating note for note and word for word. If you overdo this, it will sound like copying. This attracts negative comparison and if your song becomes commercially successful, someone's lawyers may come knocking.

Measure Your Progress

Whether you want to write a hit song, a song only for your church, one that receives a million streams or one that only you will ever hear, you must define your success. Make a list of seven ways in which you've made progress that you know you can measure.

In It To Win It

There are smaller awards and charts you can win with less competition; start there. Learn the timelines, conditions and deadlines for the ones that apply to you, enter them and then work your way up to winning bigger awards and higher chart positions. Keep your ears open to music trends; some will come and go, but others will never change.

CHAPTER 7
HOW TO GET INSPIRATION WITHOUT FORCING IT

When you break down the word inspired, you'll notice that it comes from two separate words, "in" and "spirit" — inspired. Being an inspired songwriter means to write in the Spirit. So as you write your songs, pray for the Holy Spirit to lead you, just as the Bible instructs. If we live by the Spirit, let us also keep in step with the Spirit (Gal 5:25). The Bible also teaches that God is Spirit, and His worshippers must worship in the Spirit and in truth (John 4:24). Write your songs with a heart of servitude; your best writing will be songs focused on ministering to and helping others as inspired by the Holy Spirit.

Read these three Bible verses. What do you notice about them?

- Praise the Lord. Sing to the Lord a new song, his praise in the assembly of his faithful people *(Ps 149:1)*
- Sing to the Lord a new song; His praise from the ends of the earth *(Isa 42:10)*
- Sing to Him a new song; play skillfully, and shout for joy *(Ps 33:3)*

Each verse instructs you to **sing a new song** to the Lord. The Bible is filled with verses about playing instruments, creating music and singing to God. I strongly believe that although it's great to have songs written by famous people and other worship leaders, God wants to hear **your** songs; that's why the Bible says to sing a new song. So make it your personal mission to collaborate with others in your church; together you can learn the songwriting skills in this book to sing a new song to the Lord.

Writing new songs is a fun thing to do and you're going to have times when you create with ease because you're inspired. However, other times you might feel like you're in a creative rut and cannot come up with new ideas at all. That's okay; it's fine to have off moments. When your off moments come, it's useful to have a go-to source of inspiration. So it begs the question: what is inspiration? Where do ideas come from? Where do other writers get their inspiration from? How can you get inspired when you need it most?

What is Inspiration?

In a 2014 study conducted by Frontiers in Human Neuroscience, a group of researchers studied inspiration in the creative process. They define inspiration as **a state that compels you to bring ideas into fruition**. In other words, the research shows that inspiration is not the source of your ideas. Instead, inspiration is **your response** to the idea. To phrase it differently, being inspired **by** must turn into being inspired **to** take action. So inspiration comes second and your writing comes third.

Where Do Good Song Ideas Come From?

If inspiration comes second and your action comes third, the question remains: where do good song ideas come from? Think back to chapter 1 of this book where you learned that a part of true worship is to **acknowledge God** as the one source of everything that was, that is and that is to come. It is true worship to acknowledge God as the giver of everything you've ever had, currently have and will have *(Rom 11:36, 1 Cor 8:6, Ps 24:1-3)*. In a nutshell, your best song ideas come from God because He's the source of everything. So if you'd like new song ideas, the Bible teaches to: ask and it will be given to you; seek and you will find; knock and the door will be opened to you *(Matt 7:7)*. So ask God for new song ideas as you actively seek them out, He has a lot of them to give to you.

How to Get Inspiration When You Need it Most

Before you get new song ideas, you first need new knowledge of and to experience God in new ways. The Bible teaches to draw near to God *(James 4:8, Hebs 10:22)*. As you draw nearer, God will draw nearer to you and reintroduce Himself to you again and again in different ways so that you know Him better. For example, if you pray for God to give you patience, God may expose you to new and difficult experiences — not to hurt you, but to help you practice your patience. As you experience your difficulties, you'll get to know Him as a patient God who gives patience to those who ask. That new God experience may give you song ideas that will inspire you to write and **sing a new song**.

Other biblical examples of experiencing God in new ways include:

Daniel, who thought his three friends were going to be burned alive and had a near-death experience himself with hungry lions in a den. Daniel got to know God as a fire and lion-taming God. Daniel received new experiences to write and sing a new song.

Moses, who was called to be an ambassador for God to Pharaoh and navigate the difficult politics of Egypt in setting the

Israelites free so that they could worship God. Moses got to know God as a nation-saving God who triumphs gloriously. Moses received new experiences to write and sing a new song.

David, who survived fighting a lion, a bear and a Philistine giant — all dangerous experiences that could have resulted in death — but God saved him, not once, not twice, but many times. David got to know God as a Saviour God who gives the victory. David received new experiences to write and sing a new song.

As shown in the three examples, you can only worship God to the extent that you know Him. You can't truly worship God as a deliverer if you haven't experienced his deliverance; it's just a song. You can't truly worship God as your doctor if you haven't experienced his healing; it's just a song. You can't truly worship God as your provider if you haven't experienced his generosity; it's just a song.

Put simply, you cannot worship God beyond your knowledge and experience of Him, so if you want inspiration to write songs and worship God deeper, you need to get to know Him deeper through your experiences. Start by counting your blessings; think back about how much God has done for you, how He has helped you, saved you, provided for you and protected you and how He's kept you alive when just yesterday more than 150,000 people died around the world. Read your Bible, pray and spend time with others who share your faith. Inspiration for your new songs is everywhere, and it's constant. Knowing all of this, what does it inspire you to write next?

Others as Your Source of Inspiration

One of the most instant forms of inspiration available to you is to write about the experiences of other people you may or may not know. In this style of songwriting, you become a documentary songwriter, retelling stories from your perspective. A different source of inspiration is collaborating with other spirit-led songwriters who are more experienced than you. Use the Music Matrix you learned about in chapter 2, as well as the "Give Your Worship" Facebook group to find these kinds of writers. And remember that although you may have a finished song, your song may only be half-finished. Your spirit-led collaborator could be inspired by the Holy Spirit to write the other half that makes your song complete; you may also be the other half to someone else's song.

Where Do Other Writers Get Their Inspiration From?

A very easy temptation for you as a writer is to believe that other songwriters have a magic silver bullet that helps them write awesome songs that everybody seems to connect with instantly. I want to assure you there is no magic secret; in fact, all the techniques they use — such as collaboration, personal and God experiences, pronouns, rhymes and syllables — you're learning in this book. The only difference between them and you is that they may have written more songs and really paid attention to the small distinctions that make a song succeed or fail. When you practice those same techniques, again and again, you will also start to notice and pay attention to those small distinctions that achieve your desired result.

From working with different kinds of Christian musicians, I've seen that both positive and negative experiences can inspire to write songs for the glory of God. Christian songwriters got their inspiration from the same place that you will - from God. Some of the inspiration for famous songs came from experiences and feelings of:

- Happiness
- Anger

- Sadness
- Fear
- Love
- Liking
- Disliking

It's not always rainbows and butterflies; some experiences are agonising and painful. But these Christian lyricists, musicians and worship leaders know that all things work together for the good of those who love the Lord *(Rom 8:28)*, and so they write from that perspective during good and bad experiences. They also acknowledge the emotions they're feeling, but are not overcome by them because believers are called to worship God not emotionally, but to worship in Spirit and in truth. As a result, if you've ever gone through a similar God experience as a songwriter who chose to be lyrically vulnerable, you will relate deeply with those lyrics because you know God in that capacity, also. That's part of the reason why you play your favourite songs on repeat.

Here are two stories of famous songs and where the writers received their inspiration:

***Oceans* by Hillsong:** This song was written by Matt Crocker, Salomon Leighthelm and Joel Houston. Matt was inspired and started the song with *Oceans* as a working title; all he knew was that the theme of water would play a central role in the song, but not very much more than that.

As a part of Hillsong's 2013 *Zion* album, Matt and Joel locked themselves away in a New York apartment for ten days to just write. Matt wrote the verse for *Oceans*, but couldn't write past that point. A fourth collaborator, music producer Michael Chislett, heard the early potential of the song and continued to develop and encourage the recording even though the lyrics were not yet finished.

A while later in Australia, Matt asked Salomon — a gifted storyteller and songwriter — to help with the lyrics. Salomon heard this song as a lyrical parallel of Peter on the water with Jesus as a metaphor for the song, so Matt and Joel now knew what the song would be about and that they needed to translate that biblical metaphor into lyrics.

Several months later, Matt and Joel reconnected in Australia to finish writing *Oceans* as the last song on the *Zion* album. In their words, "the lyrics just came, a song about stepping into the unknown, a song about faith, and raw trust," and the bridge section came instantly out of nowhere. A fifth collaborator, Taya Smith, was asked to sing the song on the recording just to see how she would sound, and as she sang in the studio, the team instantly knew that it was the right fit; her vocals were recorded in one take.

***Ever Be* by Bethel Music:** This song was written by Kalley Heiligenthal. The chorus was created spontaneously by Kalley who was leading in a worship room and quickly needed something repeatable that people could sing towards the end of their time of worship.

Later, when she was thinking about developing the chorus into a full song, she heard God speak to her saying that He gave her the chorus and the bridge as a "freebie," so that together they can go digging for the reasons why His praise will forever be on her lips.

That started a long process of Kalley writing several versions about why His praise will forever be on her lips. She collected and wrote down a list of reasons over the course of a year, filling every page in her notebook. Kalley knew in her heart who God is and had stories from her experiences to back it up, but could not find the words to articulate His faithfulness, His love and His Commitment to her over the years.

Because Kalley drew closer to God proactively, God drew closer to her, and with God's help, they uncovered Kalley's heart. The rest of the lyrics of *Ever Be* are something that comes from a deeply resonant and vulnerable place within Kalley. Over the years, she has known God as a covenant-keeping God who continually remained committed to her.

In Kalley's words, "I wasn't loving, I wasn't peaceful, I wasn't faithful, but because of what He did, He's making me like Him. And all of a sudden, I am faithful, I am loving, I am peaceful, I have joy, I become the things that I wasn't because of what He did." The song's key message is His praise will forever be on her lips regardless of what she's going through.

Do You Wait or Do You Write?

There are two approaches among songwriters — those who wait for inspiration before they write and those who write first and then later receive inspiration. You must decide for yourself which approach makes you a better writer and gives you consistent results. Professional writers write first, despite how they feel because faith without works is dead *(James 2:26)* and they listen as the Spirit leads. You will do well to follow their example.

So now you know the following:

- God is the source of your song ideas
- Being inspired is to be in the Spirit
- You will feel most inspired when you get new ideas

- To get new ideas, you need new knowledge of and new experiences with God
- A sense of inspiration (a.k.a. the Spirit) will move you to write songs

Your inspiration won't look the same every time, it can come in these different ways:

God. You may hear His voice; you may sense His presence and get instructions; you may witness a miracle or move of God — all of which inspire you to write songs. Learn to see, hear and sense in the Spirit to get inspiration from what God is doing.

Your personal life and God experiences are an endless source of tension, reward and inspiration as you go through seasons. When you write from your God encounters and blessings, your worship is able to release blessings, break chains and bring a healing from God to those listening.

Your Bible. Great songwriters are also great readers. Understanding the word of God will invite new and deeper revelation, so it's essential to make reading your Bible a part of your daily prayer routine. You can do no wrong writing your lyrics entirely from scripture. It's inspiration that's fast and free.

Other people who you may or may not know will also have experiences in their personal lives, as well as God encounters. You may witness firsthand or hear about their stories, which might give you new ideas and inspiration to write about, so practice your active listening skills during conversations.

Creation is very inspiring. Oftentimes, going for a walk either alone or with a songwriting collaborator can kick start your creativity. Many writers find inspiration in nature. So try writing somewhere that you can appreciate God's creation in all its different forms. Even if you're not a "nature person," there's just something about water, earth, wind, wildlife, skies and trees that induces awe and creativity.

Inspiration Hacks

These are other simple inspiration hacks that I have seen to work that you may want to try:

- Change your environment
- Play a different instrument when writing
- Write a song in a different key than normal
- Listen to the verbiage people use (especially your ideal listeners)
- Listen to new types of music
- Journal your thoughts
- Experiment without a deadline
- Exercise
- Long showers
- Quiet time to think
- Long haul travel such as flights and road trips
- Pay attention to spontaneous worship moments and record them on your phone

Start paying attention to what inspires you. It might be family, God, your passions or a certain group of people. It's going to be unique to you. Once you know what inspires you, your job will become to take yourself to those places, with those people and to do those activities as often as you need to get new ideas and inspiration.

KEY POINTS FROM HOW TO GET INSPIRATION WITHOUT FORCING IT

Inspiration and the Holy Spirit Are One and the Same

To be inspired means to be "in spirit." Start with prayer and invite the Holy Spirit into your writing session.

Sing a New Song

The Bible teaches us to sing a new song to the Lord.

Understand What Inspiration Is

Inspiration is a state that compels you to turn your ideas into reality. However, inspiration is **not** where your ideas come from.

Understand Where Ideas Come From

God is the source of all your ideas. To get inspiration and new song ideas, you need new knowledge of God and new God experiences. You can only worship God as deeply as you know Him, but no further.

Others Who Are Inspired - a.k.a. In the Spirit - Can Inspire You, Too

Get around these kinds of people, songwriters or not. Remember that if your song was inspired by breaking bondage, being blessed or receiving salvation, you also release that grace and activate that faith for listeners.

The "Big Names" Don't Have a Magic Silver Bullet

Famous writers get vulnerable and honest about the mess in their lives. They may have had more practice writing lyrics, so that's why their songs resonate. You can also be lyrically vulnerable and practice as they do.

Don't Wait, Write

Amateurs wait for inspiration. Professionals pursue the Spirit.

Hack Your Inspiration

Pay attention to what activates your inspiration. It's a unique **sequence and combination** for everyone.

CHAPTER 8
HELP PEOPLE TO SING YOUR SONGS

AUDIO

If you've been following the songwriting steps in this book, then by now you've either finished a new song, made progress on an existing song or perhaps you've got plenty of ideas for songs you want to write.

Many people will want to hear your song, learn it, play it, sing it and share it. So you may want to make it easier for them to get access to your song by creating different resources for them. This next part of the book will help you to create simple and effective recordings so your song can get out there.

Record Your Song

The most simple and effective recording of your song that you can achieve quickly and affordably is an acoustic version with just one voice and one instrument. This can be done at a recording studio near where you live, or maybe a friend who's handy with audio equipment can help you record for free.

An acoustic recording works well for several reasons:

1. It allows you to listen to your song outside of your head a little more objectively by getting near-instant feedback from listeners.

2. It helps you evaluate the strengths and weaknesses of your lyrics because if people can connect with a stripped-down version of your song, they'll also connect with a fully produced version.

3. It reveals any lyrics you may need to rewrite (tongue twisters, clumsy lyrics, unexplained details) and whether to go all-in on your song with a larger studio production budget.

The opposite is also true. If your song is not well written lyrically or melodically, no amount of top-notch studio production will make it sound any better; the studio simply amplifies what's already there.

You can take two approaches to record your acoustic song. Both are straightforward, affordable and relatively fast, however, only one approach gives you the most flexibility. The two approaches are recording with or without a metronome, also known as a "click track."

Metronome / Click Track

The first approach is recording **without** a metronome; this will give you the fastest result at an affordable price. This is ideal if you're on a very tight budget; you can be in and out of the studio within two hours if you practice. The second approach is recording **with** a metronome. This will take two to four hours of studio time to finish and give you the most flexibility for your song in the future. I always recommend that you record **with** a metronome; it's a skill worth learning that will serve you well in every studio around the world.

Something you should be aware of when recording with click tracks is to make sure the click track sound cannot be heard in the final recorded version of your song. Click track "bleed" as it's known, happens when the click track sound from the headphones is too loud and gets recorded by a microphone. It's usually the job of the music producer to ensure this doesn't happen, but keep an open ear in case he or she misses it. Although it's not the end of the world when this happens, a loud click track has the potential to ruin your awesome acoustic song. You can hear an example of "click track bleed" in the closing seconds of Lauren Daigle's acoustic version of *In Christ Alone* on YouTube.

Tip: Download a free metronome app on your phone. Practice playing your instrument to a click **without** singing. Doing this will help you keep time in a predictable way as you play. It gives you the most flexibility because it allows you to record your vocals separately and add more tracks easily in the future.

If you've practiced and simply cannot play your instrument to a click track (this can happen for some), it's best to ask a musician friend of yours (or hire a session musician) to play the instrument for you. This gives you the breathing room to focus only on your vocal performance.

Studio Time

If your song is up to four minutes long with only one instrument and one vocal, your acoustic song should take between two to four hours to record, edit, mix and master in a commercial studio. The following factors will make your recording time longer:

- If your song is longer than four minutes
- Adding a second instrument and a second vocal or more
- Not practicing and improvising new ideas last-minute
- Being indecisive about which of your takes to use

- Technical studio problems
- An inexperienced sound engineer or music producer
- Being overly self-critical of your vocal or instrumental performance

The first five points are in your control; the last two points are not. My advice is to focus on what you can control and let your sound engineer/music producer do the rest. Also, if you suffer from indecision, ask the studio professional or invite a friend who's musical as a second opinion. My experience has shown that people who are new to recording find it hard to stay objective about their performance, so a second set of ears will help you.

Practice and Preparation

You will need to follow certain steps to help ensure your studio recording session is successful:

Day 1: Practice your song for 30 minutes to a metronome

Day 2: Book your studio session

Day 3: Practice your song for 30 minutes to a metronome

Day 4: Rest

Day 5: Practice your song for 30 minutes to a metronome

Day 6: Rest

Day 7: Recording day; warm-up your vocals for 15 minutes as you drive to the studio

Tip: Practice your singing with a vocal / singing app on your phone; they are usually free or very affordable. Practicing in this way will help the muscle memory in your vocal cords to remember the correct way to sing your song.

If you've chosen someone else to sing and record your song, make sure they also practice using these suggested steps, especially if you're paying for the studio session.

While in the studio, aim to record each part in 3 to 5 takes but no more than 7 takes. This is easily doable if you follow the practice schedule mentioned earlier. Also, take an external memory device such as an 8GB USB thumb drive to save your audio files. Alternatively, you can save it to the Cloud to later download.

It is possible to record and commercially release an entirely acoustic album, and this is something to consider. Following these steps will allow you to record, edit, mix and master your acoustic song within two to four hours per song and help you to stay on budget.

Studio Recording Cost

To find out how much it will cost to record a four-minute acoustic song in a professional studio, search online for "recording studios near me." Call, email or message a local studio to find out what they charge per hour. Multiply their hourly rate by two and four, which will tell you the minimum and maximum amount per song for your budget. For example, if the studio charges 70 per hour in your local currency, multiply 70 by 2 and 4; this means your budget will be between (70x2) 140 and (70x4) 280 to record one 4-minute song, plus any local taxes.

Be sure to let the studio or producer know you are recording a simple acoustic song with one voice and one instrument. Repeat this conversation with three or more other local studios to compare prices. Next, book a session at the studio where you like the sound quality that matches your budget.

It is important to hear examples of music recorded by producers in that studio to get an idea of what result you'll be paying for. These music examples are usually posted on the studio's or producer's website and their social media; if not, ask them to email or text you links of examples.

If you follow the steps, you'll soon have a recorded acoustic song that people can listen to and enjoy. If you ignore these steps, you can expect to arrive unprepared; you'll make more mistakes, it will take longer to record, it will cost more than you budgeted and you likely won't like the sound of the final result.

Save Your Song

In addition to receiving your "final mix," ask your music producer to give you the click track, vocal tracks and instrument tracks separately as **"unprocessed WAV files at 44.1kHz / 24-bit"** format. Save them to your USB thumb drive or cloud storage like Google Drive. It will give you the flexibility to reuse those recordings in a fuller production in the future with any producer.

These steps will work whether you are recording with an instrument such as an acoustic guitar, non-acoustic instruments like an electric guitar or keyboard, and even a pre-recorded backing track. The main idea is to get your song recorded and out there.

Critical Times in Your Song

Depending on what genre you write in, the ages of your intended listeners and the devices on which they listen to your song, there are critical times during your song that you must understand and respect as a songwriter with recorded music.

The first thing to understand and accept is that your song will never be liked by 100% of people. To think that everyone will love your song is a guaranteed way to set yourself up for 100% failure. This was covered earlier.

The second thing to understand is the most critical times in your song, which include:

- **5 seconds in:** 24.14% likelihood of listener skipping

Listeners will size up your song and decide whether to listen longer or not in the first 5 seconds. Don't waste time with a long, self-indulgent introduction. Do keep it short. Slower songs are at risk of having longer intros. If so, it's okay to hum or use a vocal or instrumental adlib during your intro to compel a listener to listen longer.

- **10 seconds in:** 28.97% likelihood of listener skipping

Well done! Those who haven't yet skipped at this point liked your introduction enough to listen longer. They're now waiting to hear the melody of the lead vocals and your relatable God-focused lyrics. You have 10 seconds to captivate. I always insist that lead vocals feature at the 10-second mark or 15 seconds, MAX.

- **30 seconds in:** 35.05% likelihood of listener skipping

If your listeners have made it this far, your lyrics are relatable and they're likely listening to verse 1. Again do not overindulge with a needlessly long verse, do keep your verse between 8 to 16 bars long or any length that tells the most detail and gets to your chorus in the least time. Past the 30-second mark means listeners are actually paying attention to your song unfold, and because you're equipped with new songwriting techniques, you've captivated them for Christ with your biblically-based and detail-rich lyrics. Now they are ready and want to hear a good chorus.

- **60 seconds in:** likelihood of listener skipping FALLS drastically

Understand and accept that you **must** introduce your chorus at the 60-second mark (or earlier) or you risk losing the listener's attention. The chorus is a sort of musical "reward" that listeners love and expect to receive at a scheduled time, so make sure you deliver it on time. And when it arrives, delivering your song's key message, it satisfies the expectation of your listeners who by now should firmly have their fingers off that dreaded skip button.

The first 60 seconds are the most crucial in your recorded song, and it's your responsibility as the lyric writer to keep people engaged for all 60 seconds; this is a must. If you can get your target listeners past the 60-second mark, they are highly likely to listen to the entire song, not skip, listen again on repeat and share it with their friends. In short, you increase the likelihood of people connecting with God.

In total, 48.6% of (first-time) listeners are very likely to skip your recorded song before it finishes and that's okay. Your lyrics, however, should be well crafted so they connect powerfully and keep the remaining 51.4% of listeners engaged. When you use all the writing techniques you've learned to this point, listeners will connect. Those who don't connect the first time may connect on the 5th, 6th or 7th time as the song "grows" on them. But don't rely on those chances because you may not get them; your song has to do the hard lyrical work of connecting the first time every time. Are you starting to see how powerful this is? I hope so.

I have chosen to only focus on recording acoustic songs in this section and not to go into depth about recording a single, an EP or an album. That way, this book stays focused mainly on writing great lyrics. Perhaps another book may follow in the future titled *How To Record God-focused Songs in any Genre.* Next, let's learn about simple videos and how you can use them to connect with different people.

VIDEO

Lyric Videos

As well as hearing the audio, some people will want to read the lyrics as your song plays. Luckily, you can create free lyric videos using video editing software that comes free with your personal computer, such as iMovie on Apple computers and Movie Maker for Microsoft computers. There are plenty of free tutorials on YouTube about how to use each one; stick with it because the learning curve is short and it's super easy to do.

If you don't have these video editing software programs on your computer, you can download them for free from the App Store or the Microsoft Store. Also, both iMovie and Movie Maker are available as mobile apps to create lyric videos on your phone or tablet. However, you may find creating a lyric video on your phone a little too fidgety, which can cause frustration. For this reason, I recommend creating one on your desktop computer or laptop. Once created, simply upload your video complete with artist name and song title to video sharing websites.

The other option is to ask a friend or relative who's handy with technology to help you make a lyric video. If you can't find one, you can pay someone to do it very affordably on websites such as Fiverr.com or freelancer.com. Just type "lyric video" in the search bar and see the many budget-friendly options that appear. Choose a freelancer who has a lot of good reviews and send your song and lyrics to him or her; a few hours or days later, they will respond to you with a finished lyric video.

The key with lyric videos is to keep it simple. Your video can literally be a black background with white text, and there are plenty of examples of lyric videos like this on YouTube, such as *Broken Vessels* by Hillsong. Alternatively, you can use a white background with black text — simple. If you have the time, budget and/or passion for a more fancy looking lyric video, then go right ahead and create one. Just make sure the lyric video doesn't distract from your song's message. Good lyric videos should support and amplify your song's message and should not impress, dazzle and stun people with visuals that entertain but doesn't impact.

Lyrics in Video Description

One thing I recommend is that you always add your lyrics in the video description section on YouTube, Facebook, Tik Tok and any other video sharing websites. Why? Search engines cannot search for keywords on videos, so you must also type or paste them below every video you upload. This helps to make your song very findable by those who remember just a line of lyric and then go searching online. Search engines such as Google, Yahoo and Bing also like when creators add useful information about their song for people to find.

The video description section should contain the following:

1. **Bolded** or ALL CAPS labels above each song section (e.g. **Verse**, CHORUS, etc)
2. Your lyrics
3. Copyright symbol, year and artist name (Example: © 2020, Jon Fraiser) at the bottom of the video description

Videos That Teach

You may choose to go a step further and record a separate tutorial video that teaches both the chord names, fingering and playing techniques of your song. This is especially useful for those who learn by seeing and doing. These kinds of listeners are those who will want to play your song at church, in concert and other events.

Teaching videos are a little more involved than simple lyric videos. However, when your songs are broken down, explained and taught, they'll become very popular with guitar, keyboard, bass and lead guitar players who will teach them to other musicians.

Your teaching video doesn't have to be an elaborate production; you can use your smartphone to record the video as one continuous video with super simple edits or record multiple takes which zoom in on both hands as they play the instrument so that other musicians can see your chords and playing technique.

LYRICS, CHORD CHARTS AND MANUSCRIPT (THE EASY WAY)

In addition to your acoustic recording, lyric and tutorial video, another key component to help people sing your song is to create a lyric sheet, chord chart or music notation. This is useful for those who learn music by reading as they perform it. If you're like me and you don't read or write music very well or not at all, get a friend who's musical to help you with these next steps.

You can create a lyric sheet and chord charts for free with software such as Microsoft Word for PC users, Pages for Mac users or Google Docs online. Your lyric and chord chart should have the following parts in the top left section of your page:

- Song Title
- Artist Name
- Song Key

- Tempo
- Time Signature
- Full Song Structure (e.g. C/V/C/V/B/C)

The main body of the page should contain:

- Bolded labels at the top of each section
(Example: **Intro, Chorus, Verse 1...**)
- Your lyrics
- Chords and bass notes written over your lyrics

The footer of the page should display:

- Copyright symbol, year and songwriter's full name,
(Example: © 2020 Jesse Carter)

Once you've created your lyric and chord chart sheet, export and save it as a PDF document, so your formatting looks the same on every device. Do not save it as a Microsoft Word or text document because it will change your formatting when people open your file on their phones and computers and won't be able to use them. To see and copy this layout example of lyric and chart sheet, just search online for a song by name with chords.

If you or your church use these paid apps and you have login access to Song Select, Praise Charts or Services by Planning Centre, you can use them to create chord charts on your desktop computer. A bonus of using these apps is the ability to easily change the key of your song at the touch of a button. These apps can also make your song available to other churches, worship leaders and Christian musicians around the world to use in their Sunday services.

Next, upload your chord chart to a free cloud storage service like Dropbox and Google Drive, then copy, paste and label the URL link (Example: "chord charts") in the video description section of social media. This way, people will know where to find your chord charts. Paste this information anywhere your song or lyric video is shared such as SoundCloud, YouTube, Facebook, Tik Tok and Instagram.

Musical Notation

Some musicians can only learn music and play it by reading the music notes off music manuscript paper. These musicians are usually people who had formal music training growing up and find it a challenge to "play by ear" or improvise music without it written down.

As long as your acoustic song is recorded, some musicians can turn your acoustic recording into music notation either for one instrument or for a full band. You can easily find these types of musicians on websites like fiverr.com and freelancer.com for an affordable price. They'll ask you to send them an mp3 recording of your song and lyrics. A few hours or a few days later, they'll send you back one or multiple PDF documents of your song written on manuscript paper in glorious music notation.

A bonus of music notation is the ability to sell it online for as little as a dollar or even more. So between your acoustic recording, lyric and tutorial video, as well as chord chart and notation, you'll have all your bases covered to help as many different kinds of people learn and play your music immediately.

SOCIAL MEDIA SHARING

Social Media Numbers

A quick word about your social media numbers: it can be addictive to want your views, shares, likes and comments to go up, up, up. I recommend to all my clients that they not spend their time watching numbers or reading positive and negative comments. I suggest that you don't spend your time there, either. I have found that it makes you focus on the wrong things and can inflate or deflate your enthusiasm, confidence and self-esteem based on the wrong or unqualified **opinions** of others.

Just remember that God put that song on your heart to be expressed and it may have been a message only intended for a certain number of people to hear and be impacted. So don't be distracted by the wrong "vanity" metrics of likes or plays. Instead, pray that your song reaches and impacts the intended people for God, which social media cannot measure.

Even with this good advice, I know that some of you will ignore it and look at the metrics. So here are some percentages you can expect to see per 1,000 views or listens. As an example, if your song is purchased, viewed or listened to online by 1,000 people, then engagement levels (likes, comments or shares) may look like the examples below. Sometimes these percentages are bigger or smaller based on different factors, but in general, you can use this example as a rough benchmark per 1,000 views/ listens:

- 0.3 - 3% engagement, 3 - 30 people (Good)
- 4%+ engagement, 40+ people (Very good)
- 7%+ engagement, 70+ (Excellent)
- 10%+ engagement, 100+ (Superb)

To illustrate this further, here is a Facebook example of the song *What A Beautiful Name* by Hillsong on the "Christian Music" page at the time of writing this book:

1. Views: 2,400,000 (Excellent)
2. Likes: 85,000 = 3.5% (Very Good)
3. Shares: 71,000 = 2.9% (Good)
4. Comments: 3,100 = 0.13% (Okay)

I listed these metrics in that order because this is the descending order of engagement for most content online, with views/streams always being the largest number and comments always being the smallest. My observation over time has been that those who take all four actions (view, like, share and comment) on your music are the people who are most impacted, and sometimes most offended by your song. Bear in mind that there are also people who will play your song on repeat, causing your views to increase over time. Those who comment negatively are usually not your target listeners, meaning your song wasn't intended for them. The majority of viewers will watch and not comment at all and that's also okay.

Going Viral

I hesitate to write this next part because it's not the focus of the book, but from years of experience of working with musicians, I know that many reading this book will want to know about "going viral." The first and most obvious question is: "How do you measure going viral?" How many views does it take to go viral? The honest answer is there's not a "one size fits all" way of measuring.

However, most experts seem to agree that going viral is when a piece of content spreads very quickly and very widely in a very short amount of time. For example, if your song reaches 350,000 views over 6 years, that's not "viral," whereas if your song reaches 100,000 views in 6 hours, that's viral.

Because there's no "one size fits all" on going viral and experts don't agree 100% on the numbers, I've broken it down into different "tipping points" for ease of use. If your song or lyric video reaches these numbers in a 3 to 7 day period, it means that it went viral at that tipping point. But going viral in and of itself should not be your goal: obedience to God and writing God-focused lyrics that impact people should be your goal. The tipping points are as follows:

- 1,000
- 10,000
- 100,000
- 1,000,000
- 10,000,000

Sometimes going viral is something that happens naturally (each person who hears your song shares it with 1 to 3 people), and sometimes going viral is planned (people spend time, effort and money) to take their song to the next viral tipping point. I hesitated to write this section of the book because you may be the tempted to believe that if your song doesn't go viral in 3 to 7 days, then it's a "failure." This is not true. Your song could reach any of these tipping points in 3 to 7 weeks, 3 to 7 months or 3 to 7 years. The message here is to focus on making an impact for God first. Going viral is only a byproduct.

In the chapter that follows, we will look at at the cool and crazy things people will say about your song, the correct mindset you need to have and what to do in each scenario.

KEY POINTS FROM HELP PEOPLE TO SING YOUR SONGS

Record Your Song

An acoustic recording of your song could be the only release you need.

It Can Be Fast and Affordable

You can record an acoustic version of your song in as little as two to four hours in a professional studio or with a talented and helpful friend for free. Compare prices at three to five studios near you and choose one that fits your budget and desired result.

Share Your Song as Many Ways as You Can

People are different. Some learn by seeing, some by hearing and some by doing. So for the readers write your lyrics down, for the doers create tutorial videos and chord charts, so they can play along and for the listeners, record an acoustic version of your song complete with a lyric video. This will cover all your bases.

Data Makes Discovery Easy

Add as much data as you can in the video description sections online. It helps you, it helps the search engines and it helps the people looking for your songs.

Avoid Social Media Mania

Don't focus on things that don't matter — like vanity numbers of social media or the negative minority in your comments. Focus on making a significant impact for God through well-written songs. Social media doesn't measure this sort of impact.

Going Viral Can Be a Downward Spiral

There's no hard and fast rule about "going viral." It's nice if it happens naturally and if you have some marketing budget to reach more people with the gospel, that's great. Never attach your identity, self-esteem or confidence to the things people do or say. Attach your identity where it belongs — in Christ alone.

CHAPTER 9
CRITICISM: WHAT WILL PEOPLE SAY?

If you have been following the steps in this book, by now, you may have an acoustic recording of your song available for people to stream, learn and maybe even purchase.

At this point, it's useful to be aware of the range of reactions, which are coming your way after you upload and share your song. It's also wise to know the correct mindset towards those reactions and how best to respond.

Handle it Like a Champ

If you don't use this method of understanding, analysing and correctly responding to reactions about your songs, you will get frustrated, offended and even angry with people — possibly straining good relationships needlessly. You may get discouraged and give up on songwriting altogether and that would be a shame. But if you follow these steps, you'll understand how to separate your art from you, the artist. You'll understand how to turn reactions into better songwriting, which will impact people in life-changing ways through your music ministry.

The first step in getting feedback is to think about your personality type and how **you** typically react to challenges. For example, what does it look like when you react positively to a situation? How about when you react in a neutral way to a challenge? What are your tendencies when you react negatively to a problem? Doing this simple thinking exercise will help you to respond in an appropriate way to feedback and criticism.

This exercise will help you avoid injuring your ego from quick overreactions. It will also help you avoid an emotional implosion by underreacting and help you to keep going when you want to quit. I'm saying this: be patient with people and learn to compensate them for their feedback — not with money, but a gracious **response** (active and mindful) and not a knee-jerk **reaction** (passive and mindless).

What Will People Say?

From experience with countless music clients in the studio, on stage and on social media, I've made some observations about what people will say to you. This applies whether they're strangers, family or friends. I use a framework of only five things people typically say, but there are no absolutes, so you may get a mixture of reactions at the same time. At that point, it's your job to translate what the feedback means by either asking more questions of your listeners or putting their feedback into one of these categories. The five reactions include:

1. No reaction at all

This is the reaction you'll probably experience the most, which is no reaction at all. The best way to think about this is to assume that people have listened to your song and they like it but are too busy to respond. And that's okay with you. Avoid soliciting people who don't have time, don't know how or don't want to give you feedback. In other words, don't be a nuisance, or people will start avoiding you. If they give you any feedback, it will be low-quality and won't help you or your songwriting. The best thing for you to do is go about writing an even better song that will connect with people and point them to God.

2. Constructive feedback

This is my favourite kind of response, especially if it comes from intended listeners such as Sunday school children, non-believers and churchgoers. The best way to think about this feedback is seeing that someone went out of their way to really think about what **specific** things they like or didn't like, what works and doesn't work in your songs and then took the time to provide their feedback. A small clarification: constructive feedback won't always feel good, but it's actionable information that helps to improve your songwriting. The best response is to thank people who give constructive feedback and consider how to use that information to improve your current and next song. Then go about writing an even better song that will connect with people and point them to God.

3. Positive reaction

This reaction is what you may want to hear every time, and the challenge is to stay positive even when it doesn't come. However, remember that you're writing songs for bigger reasons than people's approval; you're writing songs for a purpose. Some people are super positive and overreactive in a good way in almost all situations. Ask them specifically what they liked about your song so you can do more of what works. If you play and sing live, it's common for people who you don't know to give you positive reactions for your song, performance and worship leadership. Don't shoot down their compliments by interrupting them mid-sentence with a list of all the mistakes you made **(which they never noticed)** or what you wish you could have done better. The only correct response is to thank them; and after you've done that, go about writing your next song that will connect with people and point them to God.

4. Neutral reaction

This reaction is neither positive nor negative; this may be because the person doesn't want to risk offending you, so they choose to stay quiet. It could also mean they are not the target listener, so they don't connect with your song or the genre. Either way, their reaction is of little use to you. If they are willing to give answers, ask them some questions to encourage useful feedback. Once you're done, go about writing your next song that will connect with people and point them to God.

5. Destructive criticism

This is the worst kind of reaction and, unfortunately, can be the most common, especially online where people can be anonymous "keyboard warriors" doing "battle" behind their screens. Not only is it negative, but it doesn't offer suggestions to improve, only opinions that tear down. These people are known as "trolls" or "haters," so avoid them. One way of understanding this is to think about how a person used up their precious time, thought and effort out of their limited day to find something to be negative about. They must be hurting real bad and really need Jesus. Don't start a war of words in the comment section; you don't belong there. If you must comment, there are two rules: 1) You only get to comment once, and 2) It must be a positive response back. If in-person, the two rules still apply with the addition of simply smiling and leaving the conversation. Once you've done that, you can go about writing your next song that will connect with people and point them to God.

Your Response

Your only response to **all** these reactions from listeners should be to thank them and use what is useful and ignore the rest. That's how you'll grow as a songwriter. You must avoid a bad reaction, such as overreacting, exploding or getting angry and telling people why they're wrong, how little they know and why you're right. Even if you're right, you'll still lose that conversation. In short, be gracious with people, especially when it's hard.

Valid or Void?

In every reaction listed, did you notice the same advice? It's true. Your response should always be to write your next best song that points people to God. I give that advice because I know that people (who are not your target listeners) will give you their opinions, which are too subjective to be helpful. They won't know how to play an instrument; they won't know about writing lyrics; they will have never recorded or released a song or even know the process, but they'll have an opinion to give to you. Although that's okay; it doesn't mean you should act on their opinions. Stay receptive to input, but take it with a "pinch of salt."

Make sure you get the opinions of the right people (your intended listeners). For example, if you write a Hip Hop song, don't ask your grandma for feedback; ask your target listeners who follow Hip Hop. If you write a hymn, don't ask your teenage cousin for his opinion; ask your target listeners who love and appreciate hymns. If you write a rock song, don't ask tiny Sunday school children what they think; ask your target listeners who are fans of rock music. That's the difference between void and valid opinions.

Remember, the **void** opinions of most people should be taken with a "pinch of salt." You didn't make music for them, so train your brain to focus more on the **valid** opinions of those who God put on your heart to serve. If it connects with them and connects them to God, you've done your job as the songwriter. Well done!

Self-Criticism

On the topic of self-criticism, understand that you are the

least able to assess yourself objectively. You have a **big** blind spot when it comes to seeing yourself and your work in a way that is not exaggerated, oversimplified or missing detail. So don't torture yourself with mind games of convincing yourself that your song is bad when it's good or that your song is good when it can use a little improvement. Get valid objective feedback from other people so you avoid your own delusions.

In brief, stay obedient to God without delay and write the songs that He has put on your heart as best as you can. Do not allow criticism or compliments to compromise writing biblical truth that points people to God.

HOW TO TELL IF YOUR SONG IS GOOD

If you've written a song and you're not sure if it's any good, then you may want to test it. Testing is an extra step; it's like a quality control check to make sure your song checks off before you release it.

This step of songwriting is optional, and you can choose to do it a little bit, a lot or skip it altogether. Taking this step will confirm whether your song is hitting the bullseye or if you're off. It's up to you to decide whether to test and how much to test.

Self-Testing

Your first and fastest test should be to spend a little time to determine if your song's **(key message, metaphors, imagery** or **meaning)** is opposite to, mocks or undermines what the Bible teaches. If it does any of these things, edit your lyrics to align your song with the word of God. If you skip this step and miss lyrical errors, you will be misunderstood.

Senior Leadership

The second test you can do that I highly recommend is to ask the senior pastor or youth pastor if you're a younger writer at your church for some feedback on your lyrics. He or she may not be musical and that's okay. You are simply looking for someone else's perspective as to whether your lyrics are biblical or not.

The third test is to send a rough recording of your song using your phone's voice recorder to the worship leader/pastor at your church for some musical and lyrical perspective.

Doing these three fast and easy tests can take about an hour to finish (depending on how fast people respond) and will be enough testing for most of your songs. If you want to go deeper to make sure your song **really** resonates with your target listeners, you can also do the following tests.

Live

The fourth test involves playing your songs live in-person for your intended listeners, such as Sunday school children, churchgoers and non-Christian listeners. This model of testing is more applicable if you have a small budget to pull it off. It's also more suited for those who will spend a lot of money: 1) professionally recording, 2) promoting, and 3) going on live tours. If you aren't doing any of these three things yet, you can skip the live test.

Your live test should happen in front of a small audience in a rehearsal space, a house show or at church. Gather a sample of your target listeners and distribute pre-written questions on small index cards or text the online version to their phones. Then, perform your songs live while your audience provides feedback. Give an incentive for attending and participating in the survey; do not underestimate the power of free pizza to motivate people!

Have fun with it. If real-time feedback is not practical, try having listeners answer questions during a short break in the middle of your show or before they leave. Remember to record their feedback either as a survey, audio or video.

Online

If testing your songs for a live audience is not needed or seems scary, you can take the online route as a fifth option. After uploading your acoustic mp3, you can simply text your song to people or use free websites such as Google Forms, Survey Monkey and Facebook comment sections to get feedback from your ideal listeners. Start with people you know, such as friends, family and acquaintances and then if you need it, add people who you don't know.

To find your ideal listeners online who you don't know, search for pages of musicians who have a similar genre and sound to your music. I recommend Facebook fan pages and groups as a starting point to find your potential listeners. YouTube, Instagram and Tik Tok are also alternatives; start a two-way conversation with fans on these platforms and invite them to give you feedback. Be sure to give them a survey deadline, so you get responses faster and offer a free song download or some other incentive, so they take action. You only need 20 responses from every 100 people who listen to your song. The feedback should be enough information to know whether to scale up and record a studio production of the song or to rewrite your lyrics.

"Give Your Worship" Facebook Group

Your sixth option for testing is to join the "Give Your Worship" group on Facebook. I created this group in conjunction with this book to bring together action-takers like you with other supportive Christian songwriters who want to give you constructive feedback on your songs, and you can return the favour of doing the same for their music.

Questions to Ask Your Listeners

1. What's your favourite music genre/style?
2. What is your first reaction to this song?
3. How would you rate this song 1(low) to 5 (high)?
4. Did you connect or relate to the lyrics?
5. What's not yet perfect and what would you change?
6. What platform do you use to listen to music?
7. Any other comments?

Asking these questions to enough listeners either for a song or an album will help you be more objective about and improve your song. Remember, you don't need many responses; a 7% to 20% response rate provides plenty of information to put into action.

If you take the steps in this chapter, you will massively increase your chances of creating songs that **really** resonate with your target listeners.

Remember, testing is an optional step. You can be proactive and follow the steps as listed here or be reactive by listening to what people say after you release a song and making changes then.

KEY POINTS FROM CRITICISM: WHAT WILL PEOPLE SAY

Check Yourself Before You Wreck Yourself

For whatever reason, music **really** activates and animates the emotion of those who write a song. Be **honest** with yourself and take personal inventory of your reactions. If you are emotionally super-sensitive, prone to an inflated ego or are a volatile person, you must protect yourself from yourself when getting feedback. Get an accountability partner who has permission to keep you in check if you start acting up, either on purpose or unknowingly. If you feel upset after reading that instruction, then it proves the point. Get an accountability partner.

Be Proactive

Decide two things **ahead** of time: 1) Decide you will feel empowered by information/feedback you receive to improve your songwriting, and 2) Regardless of what people say (positive or negative), you will continue to write songs as best you can to glorify God.

Get the Right Feedback

I can't stress this enough. Get the right feedback. Don't ask grandma if she likes your Holy Spirit Hip Hop song; don't ask your non-Christian friends if they like your Sunday service hymn, and don't ask your parents what they think about your Sunday school song. They are not the target listeners and will give you void feedback.

The Five Things People Will Say

Although people use different words, there are only five things that their feedback is saying to you. They usually say one or a combination of these things:

1. No feedback at all
2. Constructive feedback
3. Positive reaction
4. Neutral reaction
5. Destructive criticism

Void Feedback Is Useless to You

Asking the right questions to the wrong people will cause you to feel frustrated, offended or even angry. The right people are those you wrote the song for, they'll give you the most valid feedback.

Test Your Song

Ask your senior pastor, worship pastor and yourself the seven questions listed in this chapter. Friends and family (who are your target listeners) can help too. Leverage technology for even more feedback; remember that 7 to 20 people out of 100 is enough feedback. If 90% of listeners don't like your song, but the 10% who are your ideal listeners love it, that's a success.

CHAPTER 10
GOOD EXAMPLES AND MISTAKES TO AVOID

GOOD EXAMPLES

As you grow your skills and become more familiar with the songwriting process, you will start to see patterns of good songwriting emerge everywhere. When you reach this amazing milestone of being able to recognise, identify, analyse and explain songwriting techniques in a song, you'll also notice those patterns being used in other genres.

On the topic of other genres, you may one day find yourself co-writing with someone in a different genre than you. Because of that, this book is jam-packed with plenty of examples of well-written songs. As a bonus, I also added this section, so you have one place to reference good examples of songwriting in different genres to help kick start your co-writing inspiration.

The list below is not perfect, comprehensive or exhaustive. The songs on this list were not chosen for their popularity or number of views. They were chosen because they use several songwriting techniques you've learned in this book. Following are the songs by genre, artist name and song title:

Hip Hop
Cross Movement - *C To The* R
T Bone - *Wipe Your Tears*
Kanye West - *God Is*
Lecrae - Tell The World
Mali Music - *Let Go*

Contemporary Christian Music
Tasha Cobbs - *This Is A Move*
Israel Houghton - *Lord You Are Good*
Elevation Worship - *Oh Come To The Altar*
TRBLE Music - *You Keep On Getting Better*
Cory Asbury - *Reckless Love*

Traditional Gospel
William McDowell - *You Are God Alone*
Fred Hammond - *You Are The Living Word*
Marvin Sapp - *My Testimony*
Bri Babineaux - *Jacob's Song*
Kirk Franklin - *Something About The Name Jesus*

Rock
We The Kingdom - *Holy Water*
New Song - *One True God*
Casting Crowns - *Courageous*
Third Day - *I Need A Miracle*
7th Time Down - *Just Say Jesus*

Pop
Tauren Wells - *Citizen Of Heaven*

Lauren Daigle - *You Say*
Life Church - *The Cross Has Won*
Michelle Williams - *Say Yes*
Matthew West - *All In*

Country Gospel Music
Micah Tyler - *Different*
Zach Williams - *Chain Breaker*
Josh Turner - *Me And God*
Collin Raye - *The Only Jesus*
Blake Shelton - *Saviour's Shadow*

Hymns
Elevation Worship - *Resurrecting*
Kari Jobe - *Be Still My Soul*
Lauren Daigle - *How Great Though Art*
Pat Barrett - *Hymn Of The Holy Spirit*
Gaither Vocal Band - *Hear My Song, Lord*

Sunday School
Jana Alayra - *Treasure Quest*
Hillsong Kids Jr. - *The Greatest Commandment*
The Rizers - *Glory, Glory, Glory*
Listener Kids - *That's The Book For Me*
Bethel Music Kids - *O Taste And See*

There are different kinds of songwriters around the world who are also reading this book right now and want to collaborate with you. So, if you'd like to write in a genre different than yours, or you want to get out of a creative slump, reach out to them in the "Give Your Worship" Facebook group and see if anyone is available to co-write with you in one of the above or other genres.

MISTAKES TO AVOID

Nobody is perfect, and you **will** make mistakes in some of the songs you write. Hopefully by now, you've seen enough examples of world-famous songs that contain mistakes. This should give you hope to know that successful songs don't always get it right; despite the mistakes people still love them, they are still successful. So it's not a question of if you'll slip up, but when. Thankfully, there's grace for all of us.

However, just because mistakes are inevitable does not give you permission to write mindlessly. The big idea is to have little to no mistakes at all. To help you to avoid mistakes and write to a high standard, I've listed below some common mistakes I've seen writers make. Yes, even I've written a lot of these mistakes. While this list is not exhaustive, you'll avoid these mistakes by being aware of them and writing mindfully.

Mistakes to Avoid:

1. Lyrics are not based on the Bible
2. Pushing biblical interpretation too far to fit your song's agenda
3. Not mentioning God, Jesus or the Holy Spirit, ever
4. Writing a song once, never rewriting and thinking it's finished
5. Being over-sensitive to any feedback and getting offended
6. Disguising your procrastination as perfectionism
7. Writing a melody that's too hard or too boring to sing
8. Writing in 100% isolation with nobody else's perspective
9. Only writing songs about me, myself and I, the unholy trinity
10. Creating a melody that sounds like another song
11. Saying too many things in one song with no key message
12. Mixing metaphors that don't connect and are confusing
13. A title that does not feature in your song or an odd one-word title

14. Using filler words like yeah, ooh, aah, oh in the wrong genre
15. Trying to sound like someone else
16. Using pronouns inconsistently and pairing them wrongly
17. Using unproven song structures that don't work
18. Don't blaspheme *(Exod 20:7),* which means not to misuse the name of the Lord without reverence or respect, in false affirmations or in a way that impugns the character of God or belittles His power
19. Lyrics that create conflict, complain, criticise, condemn, curse and compare
20. Creating two song titles for one song
21. Having a random rhyme scheme with no pattern
22. Too many or too few syllables that don't fit the rhythm
23. Using void feedback from the wrong listeners
24. Letting social media inflate your ego, allowing negative comments to deflate your confidence and pleasing people as your motivation
25. Blazing a new trail that resembles nothing, has never been heard before and ignoring everything that has worked for centuries
26. Writing a song with "everyone" as your audience
27. Writing tongue twisters no one can sing, including you
28. Giving up on songs too soon instead of persevering
29. Not listening to your listeners
30. Collaborating with the wrong co-writers

As previously mentioned, this list of mistakes is not exhaustive. Although you may read the list and think, "Well, duh," remember that you now know songwriting techniques that makes this list a no-brainer. Also, remember that you may be collaborating with brand new songwriters who will make some or all of these mistakes. Luckily, you'll be there to help them see the pitfalls and prevent them from making avoidable mistakes.

KEY POINTS FROM GOOD EXAMPLES AND MISTAKES TO AVOID

Collect Good Songwriting Ideas

Now that you know songwriting techniques, you'll hear them everywhere. Start making mental notes of techniques that work well, analyse why you like them, what engages you most as the listener, and why others like them, too.

Every Genre Has Good Examples

Originality is that blend between something similar and something surprising. Don't reinvent the music wheel; listen to good examples in your genre.

Learn To Fail the Right Way

Songwriting will give you plenty of opportunities to make mistakes. And you will make mistakes. Your job is to learn how to fail. You fail the right way when you do the following:

1. Write a new song
2. Fail
3. Learn why you failed
4. Improve
5. Repeat step 1

This is called the cycle of success. Use it.

CHAPTER 11
PUTTING IT ALL TOGETHER

SECRET SONGWRITING STEPS TO GIVE YOUR WORSHIP

Wow! You've come a long way, and you've learned many secret songwriting techniques in this book. You've learned the fundamentals of writing lyrics; you've learned small songwriting tweaks that make a big difference; you've also learned techniques that you probably heard your whole life but never knew them by name.

If all this information has you feeling so dizzy with excitement that you don't know where to start, this chapter will put it all together for you. To finish writing your songs in 1 to 3 hours consistently, these are the steps to follow. Simply answer these 7 questions; each answer will clarify what you want to write about and simplify your writing process every time.

1. Who has God put on your heart to serve? Who do you feel a burning passion or a heavy burden for?

To answer this question, think back to the 5 categories of

Christian songs mentioned earlier in chapter 4. You may have one or more of the following on your heart.

God

You feel tremendous uncontainable love and passion for God and expressing your love for Him. You want to draw close to Him every day, to be in relationship with Him and to help others experience a deeper level of intimacy with God the Father, God the Son and God the Holy Spirit.

Lost

You feel a burning passion or heavy burden for the lost. You believe it's bonkers in today's day and age that there are people who have not yet heard about Jesus. How is that possible? You want to reach the lost for Christ and they occupy your thinking almost every day.

Church

You want to serve the church. You feel most passionate about encouraging, serving and helping your local or global church. You think about ministry, outreach, resources and strategies to start new churches and to grow existing ones. You feel restless seeing the church not maximising its potential for the Great Commission, and you want to help.

Story

You are captivated by people and their stories; you hear God's hand at work as they share their testimonies. You want to help them share their stories so that others can listen and build their faith or find salvation.

Self

You're going through pain, a dry season or suffering the aftermath of a difficult situation. It's not easy, and you want nothing more than for God to take it away now. The challenge you're facing seems big, but you love and serve a bigger God. The Bible teaches that all things work for the good of those who love Him; your Self Song must serve as a reminder of that for you and other believers experiencing similar hardship.

Using these 5 categories of Christian songs will help you to identify who God has put on your heart. If you're passionate about all 5, that's okay; just start with the one that's most pressing to you.

You may notice that writing a song in one of the 5 categories of Christian songs is too broad, so you have to get more specific by narrowing your focus. To make your song specific for your ideal listeners, you can narrow the listener's profile by factoring in their;

- Genre
- Gender
- Age

As an example, writing a song for the "Church" is too general. If your passion is youth ministry, you could write a contemporary Christian song for male and female listeners between the ages of 13 and 19. Here's a shortcut sentence to help you fill in the blanks.

I want to write a **[Genre]** song for **[Gender]** listeners aged **[#]** to **[#]** years old.

Step 1 narrows your focus away from trying to write a song for "everybody" which is too general (and doomed to fail) and more towards your target listeners; which in this example is a church song for young listeners. This first step alone makes the listener much easier to identify and makes your song more likely to succeed.

2. What stage of faith are your listeners in right now?

As a way to narrow and focus your lyrics a little more, use the 5 stages of faith that you learned in chapter 4. As a reminder, the 5 stages of faith include:

- Non-believer
- Beginner
- Believer
- Follower
- Disciple

Staying with the earlier example of having a passion for youth ministry, you could write a contemporary Christian song for male and female listeners aged between 13 and 19 who believe in God and attend church. This shortcut sentence will help you fill in the blanks.

I want to write a **[Genre]** song for **[Gender]** listeners aged **[#]** to **[#]** years old, who do/don't **[Believe]** in God and do/don't attend **[Church]**.

Step 2 narrows your lyrics to be more relevant to your listeners based on their stage of faith.

3. What spiritual need, desire, fear, problem, pain, milestone or experience is your listener, going through?

To narrow and focus your lyrics, even more, speak to a situation that your listeners may be experiencing or a need they have. Don't be tempted to put every situation you can think of in one song; one will do. Pay attention to and empathise with:

- Spiritual need
- Desire
- Fear
- Problem

- Pain
- Milestone

As you learned in chapter 4, this step of songwriting will give you an **endless variety** of things to write about because there's an endless laundry list of human needs and experiences. Therefore, it's practically impossible to list every situation and it's impossible for you to run out of song ideas when you choose to serve people through your music ministry.

Staying with the youth ministry example, if you have an upcoming youth event themed around praise and worship, you could write a contemporary Christian song for male and female listeners between the ages of 13 and 19 who believe in God, attend church and want to praise Him. This shortcut sentence will help you fill in the blanks.

I want to write a **[Genre]** song for **[Gender]** listeners aged **[#]** to **[#]** years old, who do/don't **[Believe]** in God, and do/don't attend **[Church]** and **[Insert Need]**.

Adding this distinction in step 3 focuses your lyrics to a need, occasion, milestone or situation that is relevant to your listeners.

4. What does the Bible teach, instruct or command on this topic? Which books, chapters or verses can you reference?

You learned in chapter 1 that your song is odd without God, so it's crucial to be biblical with your lyrics. Write your songs with an open Bible, use the Bible app on your mobile or visit www.bible.com on your computer. List Bible verses that apply to the situation you're writing for and include as much of the word of God in your lyrics as creatively possible. To keep your wording consistent, use only one Bible translation per song.

Step 4 will help you to make sure that you're always delivering the word of God to your audience. Look for specific lessons from the Bible that covers your song's topic. If specifics are not available, look for biblical principles that are relevant to the situation and is helpful to your listeners.

5. Can You Relate to Your Listener's Spiritual Need, Desire, Problem, Fear, Pain or Milestone?

Some of your best songs will be written from personal experiences that you, as the writer, have gone through. So, if you went through something relatable for your listeners, write about it. If you have not gone through certain experiences, you can still write a song that relates and connects by having open and honest conversations with your listeners about their experiences and using that as your inspiration.

Step 5 adds authenticity to your lyrics so that you can write from personal experience and not have to imagine and make things up. If you can't relate to the need, milestone or experience, then you can simply encourage your listeners.

6. Who should you collaborate with to write or rewrite your song to make it even better for your listeners?

You learned about the benefits of collaboration in chapter 2; it's your number one songwriting shortcut, so use it. When you finish writing your lyrics, stay open to the idea that although you finished, your song may only be half completed. Your collaborator could have the other half of your idea that will take your song to the next level. This happens often, so stay open to rewriting certain parts and write two versions of the same song if you're feeling unsure.

Step 6 helps you to keep going when you're having off days so that you don't quit. It also gives you someone else's experiences that listeners can relate to if you haven't gone through it yourself. Those experiences keep your song genuine and improve the quality by having two or more collaborators working on a song.

7. What's the one key message your listener needs to help them engage in worship and connect to God?

Your song should have one key message, a biblical takeaway that resonates with your listeners and addresses their need from question 3. This key message can be one of worship to God, a Godly resolve or a biblical moral to your story. The key message is usually placed in the chorus and is often the song title or the hook as you learned about in chapter 3.

Step 7 is about delivering your key message to your targeted listeners. Here you can give praise and thanksgiving to God, as well as edify and encourage listeners as they go through different seasons; both the challenging ones to endure and the great ones to enjoy.

Using these secret songwriting steps to give your worship will help you to write lyrics that connect powerfully with people who will want to listen to your song on repeat. It will help to make your message biblical and lead people to worship God, and it will help you to finish songs in 1 to 3 hours consistently the more you put it to practice. Here's a simple visual that you can use as a reminder and take with you to every songwriting session:

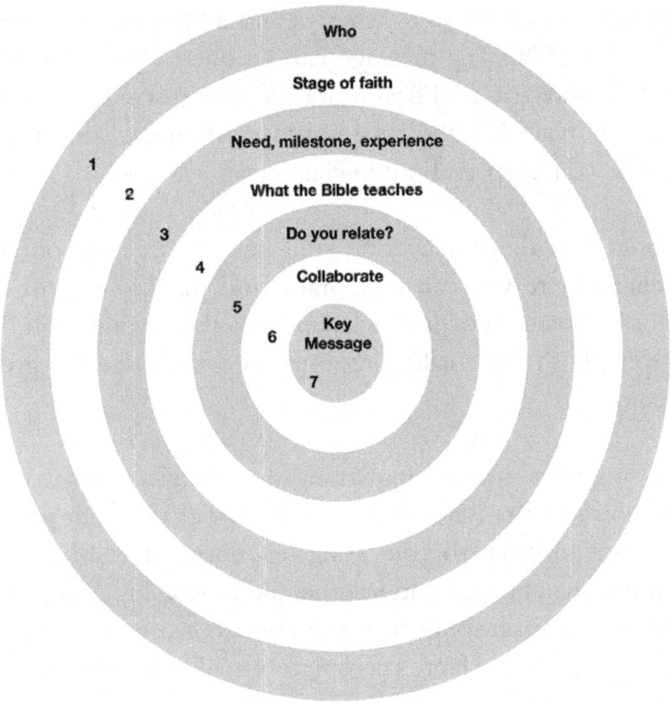

Secret songwriting steps to give your worship

KEY POINTS FROM PUTTING IT ALL TOGETHER

Use the Secret Songwriting Steps to Give Your Worship

The secret songwriting steps are designed to help you deliver your key message to your target listeners. Its a framework of songwriting that helps to give your song focus, keep your message biblical and your lyrics relatable. It will give you near-endless ideas of what to write for the people you are called to serve. The 7 questions to answer are:

1. Who has God put on your heart to serve? Who do you feel a burning passion or a heavy burden for?

2. What stage of faith are your listeners in right now?

3. What spiritual need, desire, fear, problem, pain, milestone or experience is your listener going through?

4. What does the Bible teach, instruct or command on this topic? Which books, chapters or verses can you reference?

5. Can you relate to your listener's spiritual need, desire, problem, fear, pain or milestone?

6. Who should you collaborate with to write or rewrite your song to make it even better for your listeners?

7. What's the one key message your listener needs to help them engage in worship and connect to God?

CHAPTER 12
YOUR SONGWRITING CHECKLIST

Congratulations! You've made it to the end of the book. If you've jumped straight to this page as your "shortcut" method of "finishing" this book, you've cheated yourself out of understanding crucial songwriting principles leading up to this point. So, when the frustration of creating bad songs becomes too much for you to bear, you have an open invitation to read this book from the start. Your results will reflect your actions.

It's easy to forget good songwriting practice when you're in the middle of writing. Even I sometimes forget to implement some of the techniques, tips and tricks in this book, so I often come back to re-read. I suggest you do the same. I must give credit to the late Ralph Murphy who first taught me his version of this checklist, which I have tweaked and changed so it can help you.

When you can check off as many of these items as possible, you maximise your chances of:

- Glorifying God with your lyrics
- Staying biblical

- Creating a well-written song
- Connecting with your ideal listener
- Reduce mistakes and audience misunderstanding

Your songwriting checklist includes:

1. Did you include God in your lyrics explicitly or implicitly?
2. Are your lyrics biblical in theme, message or meaning?
3. Does your melody invite your listeners in?
4. Do your words speak to a specific audience about something specific and relevant to them?
5. Do you have more than one key message? If yes, choose one.
6. Do your first couple of opening lines in verse 1 set the stage for the message to follow/story to unfold?
7. Did you properly set up the chorus by using the words (and, if, but) in your verse or by making a statement or asking a question?
8. Does your chorus (and song title) feature in the first minute?
9. Is the hook in the right place? The title hook usually occurs as the last line of your chorus, sometimes as the chorus' first line and rarely elsewhere.
10. Did you change the melody from verse to chorus to bridge?
11. Did you change rhyme scheme in your verse, chorus and bridge?
12. Have you kept your pronouns consistent?
13. Does your song build with new ear-catching layers of detail?
14. Do you use single-syllable words, or are your words long?
15. Are your lyrics consistent with what your ideal listener would hear in everyday conversation?
16. Is there a beginning, middle and end to your song?
17. Did you use one of the 7 song structures?
18. Did you explain the premise of the song?
19. Is your song easy for ordinary people to sing?
20. Is your song satisfying for your ideal listener?

Your song will stand the highest chance of success when it satisfies as much of this checklist as possible. If your song is not able to check off all these items, don't worry. It doesn't mean you have a bad song; it does, however, mean you should stay open to rewriting parts that can be improved.

KEY POINTS FROM YOUR SONGWRITING CHECKLIST

Truly Great Songs Are Not Written, They Are Rewritten

Embrace the new habit of assuming mistakes and asking questions about your lyrics. If your song creates questions, the answer should be somewhere in your lyrics.

Read your lyrics out loud without melody, as though you are reading a storybook. Do your lyrics make sense? Do they engage and build naturally? The answer should be yes. If not, it's okay to rewrite a line or two.

CLOSING THOUGHTS

The songwriting knowledge you now know did not come as easy to me as it has to you; you had the good wisdom to read this book. However, I had to learn to play instruments, earn a degree, fly around the world, find mentors who were willing to help, spend tens of thousands of dollars, and go through a lot of trial and error in music and ministry for almost two decades to learn the knowledge that you now know. You are obviously much more clever than I am, so use this new knowledge starting now.

My **ONE** goal for you through this book was to teach you how to write God-focused lyrics in **1 to 3 hours** consistently so that you can impact people for God. Because you've finished this book, I have achieved my goal. Now it's your turn to use these secret songwriting steps to impact the people that I cannot reach, but you can. So start writing now.

I'm looking forward to hearing stories from you about how God is using your songwriting talent. Tag this book on social media #GiveYourWorship and tag me @EliasLenge with all your stories. Also, when you see me at events, songwriting workshops, retreats or conferences, please say hello.

Keep writing, keep recording, keep releasing, keep worshipping and keep improving. Start now.

ABOUT THE AUTHOR

Elias Lengé first started leading worship at his home church in England when he was 14 years old. He soon developed a love for recording and has been producing music ever since. As a music producer, Elias works from commercial studios recording many languages and in several genres, including Contemporary Worship Music, Pop, Hip Hop, Country and more. He graduated from the reputable London College of Music with a B.A Honours degree in Music Technology. He collaborates with and instructs individuals and groups how to write, record, release and perform God-focused music in any genre. He lives in Calgary, Canada with his beautiful wife Jemimah Lengé. *Give Your Worship* is his first book.

HOW TO SELL YOUR SONGS

FREE BONUS AUDIO CHAPTER

To say thank you AGAIN, I'd like to give you a **FREE** bonus audio chapter called "How To Sell Your Songs."

TO GET THIS FREE AUDIO BONUS GO TO:
Https://www.GiveYourWorship.com/**SellYourSongs**

Scan With Smartphone Camera To
Download Free Bonus Audiobook Chapter

REVIEW THIS BOOK ONLINE!

Thank You For Reading My Book

I really enjoy all of YOUR feedback,
and I love hearing what you have to say.

I need your input to make the next version of this book
and my future books even BETTER FOR YOU.

Please leave me your healthy review online,
letting me know what you think of this book.

Thank you so much!

Elias Lengé

**Scan With Smartphone Camera To
Write Your Review Online**

CHORD PROGRESSIONS TO SPARK SONG IDEAS

Major Keys: C, D, F, G & A

I	IV	V
C	F	G
D	G	A
F	Bb	C
G	C	D
A	D	E

I	vi	IV	V
C	Am	F	G
D	Bm	G	A
F	Dm	Bb	C
G	Em	C	D
A	F#m	D	E

ii	V	I
Dm7	G7	Cmaj7
Em7	A7	Dmaj7
Gm7	C7	Fmaj7
Am7	D7	Gmaj7
Bm7	E7	Amaj7

I	vi	ii	V
C	Am	Dm	G
D	Bm	Em	A
F	Dm	Gm	C
G	Em	Am	D
A	F#m	Bm	E

I	V	vi	IV
C	G	Am	F
D	A	Bm	G
F	C	Dm	Bb
G	D	Em	C
A	E	F#m	D

I	IV	vi	V
C	F	Am	G
D	G	Bm	A
F	Bb	Dm	C
G	C	Em	D
A	D	F#m	E

I	iii	IV	V
C	Em	F	G
D	F#m	G	A
F	Am	Bb	C
G	Bm	C	D
A	C#m	D	E

I	IV	I	V
C	F	C	G
D	G	D	A
F	Bb	F	C
G	C	G	D
A	D	A	E

I	IV	ii	V
C	F	Dm	G
D	G	Em	A
F	Bb	Gm	C
G	C	Am	D
A	D	Bm	E

Minor Keys: Am, Bm, Dm, Em F#m

i	VI	VII
Am	F	G
Bm	G	A
Dm	Bb	C
Em	C	D
F#m	D	E

i	iv	VII
Am	Dm	G
Bm	Em	A
Dm	Gm	C
Em	Am	D
F#m	Bm	E

i	iv	v
Am	Dm	Em
Bm	Em	F#m
Dm	Gm	Am
Em	Am	Bm
F#m	Bm	C#m

i	VI	III	VII
Am	F	C	G
Bm	G	D	A
Dm	Bb	F	C
Em	C	G	D
F#m	D	A	E

ii	v	i
Bm7b5	Em	Am
C#m7b5	F#m	Bm
Em7b5	Am	Dm
F#m7b5	Bm	Em
G#m7b5	C#m	F#m

i	iv	v	i
Am	Dm	Em	Am
Bm	Em	F#m	Bm
Dm	Gm	Am	Dm
Em	Am	Bm	Em
F#m	Bm	C#m	F#m

VI	VII	i	i
F	G	Am	Am
G	A	Bm	Bm
Bb	C	Dm	Dm
C	D	Em	Em
D	E	F#m	F#m

i	VII	VI	VII
Am	G	F	G
Bm	A	G	A
Dm	C	Bb	C
Em	D	C	D
F#m	E	D	E

i	iv	i
Am	Dm	Am
Bm	Em	Bm
Dm	Gm	Dm
Em	Am	Em
F#m	Bm	F#m

REFERENCES

Links

Benediktsson, Björgvin, Radio-Ready VS Spotify-Solid (blog post), https://www.audio-issues.com/music-mixing/radio-ready-vs-spotify-solid/

Pagan, Eben, How Coaching Sells Itself, (video), https://virtualcoach.com/2019/turn-conversation-into-client/

Putman, Jim, The 5 Stages of Spiritual Growth, PDF, http://relationaldiscipleshipnetwork.com/products-page/discipleship-2/the-5-stages-of-spiritual-growth-traits-phrases-characteristics-diagram/

Moxey, John, Song Building Blocks, (blog post), https://www.songstuff.com/song-writing/article/song_building_blocks/

Moxey, John, A Guide To Song Forms - Song Form Overview, (blog post), https://www.songstuff.com/song-writing/article/song-form-overview/

Masterclass, Songwriting 101: Learn Common Song Structures, (blog post), 22 Oct 2019, https://www.masterclass.com/articles/songwriting-101-learn-common-song-structures#what-are-the-most-common-song-structures

Parker, Clifton, Stanford Research Shows That Working Together Boosts Motivation, (Report), 15 Sept 2014, https://news.stanford.edu/news/2014/september/motivation-walton-carr-091514.html

Gilles, Bobby, Songwriting Toolkit: The Verse-verse-verse hymn structure, (blog post), https://mysonginthenight.com/2013/05/14/songwriting-toolkit-the-verse-verse-verse-hymn-structure/

Wikipedia, Thirty-Two-Bar Form, (Article), 12 January 2020, https://en.wikipedia.org/wiki/Thirty-two-bar_form

Lester, G. Brooke, Psalms of lament, (blog post), https://www.bibleodyssey.org/en/passages/related-articles/psalms-of-lament

Ravenscraft, Eric, The Science of Inspiration, (and How to Make it Work For You), (blog post), 19 Nov 2013, https://lifehacker.com/the-science-of-inspiration-and-how-to-make-it-work-for-1467413542

Baas, Matthijs, The scientific study of inspiration in the creative process: challenges and opportunities (academic article), 25 June 2014, https://www.ncbi.nlm.nih.gov/pmc/articles/PMC4070479/

Wynne, Robert, There Are No Guarantees Or Exact Statistics For Going Viral (blog post), 9 March 2018, https://www.forbes.com/sites/robertwynne/2018/03/09/there-are-no-guarantees-or-exact-statistics-for-going-viral/#67e961dc5e8c

Music Machinery, The Skip, (Blog Post) 2 May 2014, https://musicmachinery.com/2014/05/02/the-skip/

Kilpatrick, Bob, How to write a really mediocre worship song, (blog post), Music Academy,https://www.musicademy.com/how-to-write-a-really-mediocre-worship-song/

https://www.billboard.com/charts

https://www.grammy.com/

https://doveawards.com

https://www.thestellarawards.com/

Books

Murphy, Ralph, Murphy's Laws of Songwriting, Murphy Music Consulting, 2013

Bolt, Chandler, Published, Chandler Bolt, 2016

ISBN 9781777170264
9 781777 170264
90000 >

Made in the USA
Monee, IL
18 October 2026

66035042R00132